LEARNING ADVENTURES!

Spring

Publisher .... *Arthur L. Miley*

Editor .... *Crystal Abell*

Art Director .... *Debbie Birch*

Illustrators .... *Fran Kizer*

Roger Johnson

These pages may be copied.
Permission is granted to the buyer of this book to reproduce, duplicate, or photocopy student materials in this book for use with pupils in Sunday school or Bible teaching classes.

Unless otherwise indicated, all Scripture is taken from the KING JAMES VERSION of the Bible.
Scripture marked (NIV) is taken from the HOLY BIBLE, NEW INTERNATIONAL VERSION.
Copyright © 1973, 1978, 1984 International Bible Society.
Used by permission of Zondervan Bible Publishers.

Portions of the *Learning Adventures* series were previously published
as part of the *Creative Church Parties* series.
Copyright © 1991 Rainbow Publishers.

Copyright 1997 • Second Printing
Rainbow Books • P.O. Box 261129 • San Diego, CA 92196

#RB36313
ISBN 1-885358-13-X

TABLE OF CONTENTS

Ages 2 & 3

Unit 1—Ages 2 & 3
Bear-y Fun Baskets 8
Little Lambs 11
Away We Go Get-Together 14
1-2-3 Go! 17
Animals and Rainbows 20

Ages 4 & 5

Unit 2—Ages 4 & 5
King for a Day 24
Irish Smilin' Time 27
Dannylions 30
Creature Convention 34

Grades 1 & 2

Unit 3—Grades 1 & 2
Joyful Jubilee 38
April Showers 41
Backward Bash 44
May Play Day 47

Grades 3 & 4

Unit 4—Grades 3 & 4
Frosty Fridge Time 50
Missions-Minded Progressive Dinner 53
Jolly Green Jubilee 56
Planting Project 59
Traffic Jam-Boree 62

INTRODUCTION

Welcome to a great time of fun and learning about God–*Learning Adventures!* The purpose of these group functions is to teach young children about the Bible. Each activity is an excellent teaching tool that complements your current classroom instruction in a fun way that involves the kids. While these action programs provide for creative play, their ultimate purpose is to reinforce lessons from the Bible.

This book is very teacher-friendly! Each book in the *Learning Adventures* series contains eighteen age-appropriate activities that will help you teach biblical concepts in a fun, adventurous way. Each activity contains the following:

- **Lesson Idea** that explains the biblical concepts that are the focus of the activity.
- **Memory Verse** to reinforce the lesson.
- **Multiple Activity Suggestions** that can be used all at once or spread out over a number of meetings to make each day special.
- **Devotions** that will help the Bible come alive for young children. These devotions are also age-appropriate and thus may be read directly to the children.
- **Reproducible Invitation** and publicity suggestions to maximize participation of the kids.
- **Decoration and Preparation instructions** that will help you easily create a fun, exciting environment for the kids.
- **Refreshment suggestions**.

These activities require only simple planning and preparation–you determine how elaborate they will be. Our hope is that this book will help you create an exciting learning environment that will reinforce biblical lessons. Have fun teaching the children about God's Word!

Ages 2 & 3

Bear-y Fun Baskets 8
Little Lambs 11
Away We Go Get-Together 14
1-2-3 Go! 17
Animals and Rainbows 20

Bear-y Fun Baskets

Memory Verse: "Do not forget to do good and to share with others." Hebrews 13:16 (NIV)

IDEA
Soft and cuddly teddy bears, pretty and practical baskets—these things combine for a fun get-together that will help you teach the children about sharing.

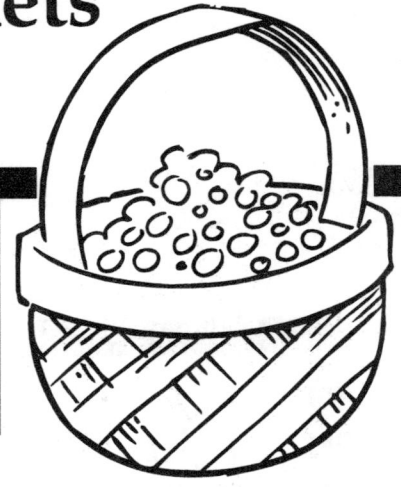

PUBLICITY
Fill in the necessary details and duplicate the invitation pattern for all the children; enlarge a copy to put up as a poster. If possible, put bear-shaped stickers on the invitations and poster.

Ask the parents to let their children bring stuffed bears to be used as part of the decorations and activities.

DECORATIONS & PREPARATION
Set up baskets and plastic honey jars around the room, "hiding" some of them for a later activity.

As the children arrive, let them "help" you find an appropriate spot for their bears to become part of the decorations. Place some bears at a table, some trying to climb, some hibernating under a blanket, and so on. Be as creative as you can. Have a few extra bears on hand for children who may not have brought one.

ACTIVITIES

Make a Bear
What you'll need: Brown construction paper, scissors, blank paper, glue sticks, and crayons

Ahead of time, cut out the following number of circles for each child to make a bear: one 4½ inch for the face, one 6 inch for the body, four 2 inch for the arms and legs, and two 1 inch for the ears.

At the party, help each student glue the circle patterns onto a blank sheet of paper. Give the children crayons to make the eyes, nose, and mouth.

Looking for Honey
What you'll need: Duplicated tree poster, tape, and bear stickers

Duplicate the tree poster ahead of time (perhaps enlarging it) and tape it on a wall at the children's shoulder level. At the party, give each child a bear sticker and tell him he will have a turn to try to help his bear find a beehive full of honey on the tree.

Have the children close their eyes and direct them to the poster board on the wall. With eyes still closed, they may place their stickers on the poster. Offer praise to all the children.

Bear-y Best Basket
What you'll need: Baskets, crackers, plastic sandwich bags, and small plastic honey jars

While the children are occupied with the previous activity, have a helper hide several sandwich bags of crackers and small plastic honey jars.

Give each child a basket and lead the group in the following rhyme:

Here is a basket I carry with me
   To hold special things that I sometimes see.
Today I will look for honey so yummy
   And crackers too—what fun for my tummy!

Into my basket they'll go right away,
   Then I'll bring them to teacher and kindly say,
"Here is my basket, full of good things.
   I can't wait to see the fun that it brings!"

As soon as a child finds an item, he is to put it in his basket and bring it to you. Let the children know how many more they still need to find. Share the yummies among the children.

REFRESHMENTS

Since the snack ties in with the devotional, you might want to plan to switch the order and begin with the Bible lesson for maximum learning benefit.

Heat up two fish sticks for every guest and serve with crackers and water or juice. After the children have completed their snack, let them pretend to fill up twelve baskets of food left over like the disciples did when Jesus fed the 5,000.

DEVOTIONS

The basket theme may be carried out through the devotional by sharing with the children the miracle of the feeding of the 5,000. Open your Bible to John 6:5-13.

Let's pretend we're climbing up a big hill. There is someone very special at the top of this hill. He has done many good things. Do you know who it might be? Yes, it is Jesus!

Jesus is talking to many, many people. He is talking about the love of God, His Father.

It's going to get dark soon and we're starting to get hungry. It would be a long walk to the village to buy food. What can we do?

Look, a little boy is talking to Jesus and His friends. It looks like he is giving Jesus a basket of food. He is sharing. Now Jesus is praying and His friends are handing out the food.

There's enough fish and bread for all of us. We've eaten until we're full, and now Jesus' friends are gathering up leftover food into baskets. Jesus has done something no one else could do.

Talk with the children about how it was good that the little boy shared his lunch. Jesus was able to use it to help many people. Name some things the children could do to share, such as letting another child take a turn playing with a toy or using a crayon.

Say the Bible verse with the children. Repeat the verse several times as you move into refreshment time. Pray with the students that God would help them remember to share.

INVITATION

PLEASE COME FOR A TIME OF

Bear-y Fun Baskets

BRING YOUR BEST STUFFED BEAR

DATE   TIME   PLACE

PATTERNS FOR DUPLICATION

Little Lambs

Memory Verse: "I am the Good Shepherd, and know My sheep." John 10:14

IDEA
Children love animals and their interest in lambs is no exception. The guests will enjoy these fun ideas, pretending to be sheep. They will also begin to learn the importance of following the Shepherd.

PUBLICITY
Fill in the necessary details on the invitation pattern and duplicate for each child.

To make a poster, enlarge the pattern and make it come "alive" by gluing cotton balls on the lamb. Cut out ears from black felt and add a dark button for a nose. If you can borrow a stuffed lamb, place it next to the poster.

DECORATIONS & PREPARATION
Make your classroom into a "yard" to keep lambs. Set up a place to graze (the area for activities), a pen to stay safe (a circle of chairs for the devotional), and a place to drink (the refreshment table). You may also want to get several different pictures of sheep for the walls.

ACTIVITIES

Lamb Headbands
What you'll need: Duplicated and pre-cut headbands, cotton balls, glue, construction paper, scissors, tape, and a stapler

Duplicate the lamb's head pattern ahead of time, making one for each guest expected. Glue these lamb heads onto construction paper to make them more sturdy. Cut out the patterns.

At the party, give each child a handful of cotton balls and put glue on the lamb. Let the children stick on the cotton balls. Cut two strips, 2 ½ by 11 inches each, from construction paper. Staple these strips to the headband and cover with pieces of tape for safety. Wrap the strips around each child's head to establish correct size. Remove the headband to staple the two ends (overlapping) and cover with tape for safety. The headband is ready to wear.

Hide the Sheep
What you'll need: Room to play

Allow the children to wear their headbands for this game, which is similar to Hide and Seek. Help one child be the hidden "sheep" while the others are in another room or are turned with their eyes covered. When he is hidden, announce to the rest of the group, "Find the Sheep." Whoever finds the sheep first gets to hide for the next round.

Follow the Shepherd
What you'll need: Items for an obstacle course such as a table, chairs, blankets, ball, empty basket, old tub, etc.

Set up an obstacle course. You can vary it according to the objects on hand; use your creativity. Ideas would be for each "lamb" to crawl under the table, squeeze between chair legs, step in a tub and pretend to have a bath, stop to eat out of an empty basket, and crawl under the blanket to go to sleep. Keep the course simple with only four or five obstacles.

Play the role of the shepherd first so the children know what to do. Go through the obstacle course several times, choosing someone different as a new shepherd each time.

The Lord Is My Shepherd
What you'll need: Accompaniment

Try to line up a pianist or guitarist to help with this activity. Have the "sheep" sit in a circle and teach them the song, "The Lord Is My Shepherd, I'll Walk With Him Always."

REFRESHMENTS

For every ten children, provide the following ingredients: 2 cups bite-size crackers, 2 cups Goldfish® crackers, 1 cup raisins, and 1 cup (6 oz.) semi-sweet chocolate chips. Place the appropriate portions in separate containers and choose several children to pour the contents into a big bowl. Allow the other children to take turns stirring up the ingredients.

With a paper cup, dish ½ cup onto each plate. Serve the "Lamb's Delight" with juice.

DEVOTIONS

Tell the children Jesus' parable of The Lost Sheep. Open your Bible to Luke 15:3-7 so the children associate the story with the Bible:

Jesus once told a story that had a very special meaning. It was a story about a shepherd who had many sheep. Every night the shepherd would count them to make sure they were all there and they were safe.

One night the shepherd was missing a sheep! What do you think he did? He went out to look for the lost sheep until he found it. Then he called his friends and neighbors together to tell them how happy he was that he found his lost sheep.

Jesus says, "I am the Good Shepherd, and know My sheep" (John 10:14). **We are His sheep. The Bible says, though, that when we disobey, we are like the sheep that was lost. The good news is that God cares for us and wants us to be safe. He wants us to be with Him all the time, and He is happy when we make good choices.**

Repeat the Bible verse with the students. Invite one of the older ones to offer a closing prayer, thanking God for being our Shepherd and caring for us.

INVITATION

Please come join the *Little Lambs*

DATE   TIME   PLACE

PATTERNS FOR DUPLICATION

Away We Go Get-Together

Memory Verse: "Blessed is the King." Luke 19:38 (NIV)

IDEA

This activity will introduce different means of travel to the children, both today's and those in Bible times. The boys and girls will also find out that one great day Jesus rode a donkey into the city and the people gave Him praise.

SCHOOL BUS

PUBLICITY

Fill in the details on the invitation pattern and duplicate for all the children.

Enlarge a copy for a poster. Place several toy cars, planes, boats, etc. next to the poster as attention-getters.

In your publicity, ask the parents to help their children bring in a toy that represents a means of transportation.

DECORATIONS & PREPARATION

Decorate the room with the duplicated pattern and magazine pictures of various modes of transportation. Have one wall representing each category: land, rail, water, and air.

If possible also bring a hat, such as a sailor's cap, that represents each category to be used in the activities.

As the children bring their toys, place them in a big paper bag.

ACTIVITIES

Toddler Travelers

What you'll need: Bag filled with children's toys (Optional: hats)

Let each child take a turn choosing a toy out of the bag. He will tell the other children what the toy is. Ask each child, **How do you play with this toy?** If you have a hat to represent the mode of transportation, let the child put on the hat before he completes his actions. If children seem inhibited, help them by taking a turn yourself.

As each child takes his turn, ask questions about places he might go. For example, ask, **Belinda, do you like to have fun at the beach?** or **Jimmy, do you like to go to the park?** Some of the older children may want to "elaborate" on their answers.

The Wheels on the Bus

What you'll need: Chairs

Line up chairs in two columns with two chairs in each column. Invite the guests to get on the "bus" and teach them this favorite nursery tune:

The wheels on the bus go round and round,
Round and round, round and round.
The wheels on the bus go round and round
As we ride to school.

Discuss what else happens on the bus and add as many verses as you wish. Some suggestions are: the door on the bus goes open, shut; the windows on the bus go up and down; the horn on the bus goes beep, beep, beep; and so on.

Which Boats Float?

What you'll need: Large bowl of water or access to a large sink, variety of toy boats and containers such as plastic margarine tubs, and square pieces of aluminum foil

Put different boats and containers into the water. Let the children guess which they think will float. Show what happens when the boat fills up with water.

Help the children make a little boat with their sheets of aluminum foil by turning up the edges. Let the students play with their boats in the water.

Red Light, Green Light
What you'll need: Red and green construction paper

Line up the children against a wall while you are across the room. As you hold up the green paper (green light), direct the children to start walking toward you until you hold up the red paper (red light) and ask them to stop moving and stand still. Play this a couple more times.

Another way to play would be to include particular means of travel. Lead the children in doing a motion related to a means of transportation, such as spreading out arms like a plane, until you say stop.

REFRESHMENTS

Make "Train Car Toast" for a fun snack. Serve a sweet-type of bread, perhaps raisin bread, with butter or margarine. Slice up a few bananas for the children to add wheels to their "train cars." Serve with milk.

DEVOTIONS

Use the transportation activities to teach about Jesus' triumphal entry into Jerusalem on a donkey. Open your Bible to Luke 19:28-38.

What was transportation like when Jesus lived on earth? The people then did not have cars, buses, trains, or airplanes. Most of the time they had to walk wherever they went, and it took a long time.

Jesus had to walk too, but one special day He rode an animal. Can you guess what it was? It was a donkey.

As He was coming close to the city of Jerusalem, Jesus told some of His friends to get a donkey for Him. They put their coats on the donkey to make a soft cushion for Jesus to sit on. Then Jesus rode the donkey into the city, and the people on the side of the road started praising Him. They waved palm branches and shouted, "Blessed is the King who comes in the name of the Lord!"

Invite the children to wave their hands in the air and say the Bible verse with you several times: "Blessed is the King" (Luke 19:38 NIV). Ask a child to pray, thanking Jesus for being our King.

INVITATION

Zoom on in for the
**Away We Go
Get-Together**

DATE
TIME
PLACE
BRING TRAVEL-TYPE TOYS

PATTERNS FOR DUPLICATION

1-2-3 Go!

Memory Verse: "God. . . loved us, and sent His Son."
I John 4:10

IDEA
Your students are at an age where counting is an interesting and fun challenge. The activities included here help children recognize 1-2-3, and the numbers will help you tell that very special message of love, the crucifixion story.

PUBLICITY
Write the date, time, and place on the invitation pattern before duplicating for your class.

For a poster, use different colors of construction paper to make big numerals (1, 2, and 3) and cut them apart. Write the details on the numerals and add a few curled ribbons for decoration.

DECORATIONS & PREPARATION
Decorate your room with single items, items that come in pairs, and items where three belong together. You may bring real items or pictures.

ACTIVITIES

1-2-3 Treasure Hunt
What you'll need: Pieces of paper, three paper bags, and "treasure" of stickers or such for children to share

Ahead of time write several clues on pieces of paper that you will read to the children to help them find the "treasure." Suggested clues could be: Clue #1—Look for me near the door of the room. Clue #2—Look for me under the table. Clue #3—Find me in a paper bag in a corner. Place the bag of treasure in the appropriate locations.

To start, divide the group into three teams; each team will be given a different clue for a different area of the room where a treasure is hidden. After telling group one their clue, send them on their way. Continue until each group has been given its clue and has found its treasure. Share the treasures found.

Things that Belong
What you'll need: Various pictures and items, some of which have a second or third just like it

If you wish, use the items you decorated with or have additional items specifically for this activity.

As you show or point to the various items, ask the children to help you decide how many you have of each item. For instance, show a paper cup and ask if the children can find any other paper cups. If there are two, put them in the pile for pairs. If you have three baseballs, set those in the pile for things in triplicate. Help the children count the sets of items in each pile.

Things that Don't Belong
What you'll need: Several groups of three items where two are the same and one is different, e.g. two oranges and one apple or two cars and one boat

Display the groups of three items. Allow the children to take turns choosing the item that doesn't belong. Let the children regroup the items.

REFRESHMENTS
Explain to the children that they are going to make a special salad with a face on it. Wash and prepare the following foods and put them in separate bowls: raisins, grapes, sliced apples, sliced bananas, and carrot sticks. Give each student a small mound of cottage cheese on a plate.

Working with one bowl at a time, say, **First we are going to use the raisins for eyes. How many eyes do we have?** Let each child take out two raisins. Carry out the idea by using one grape each for a nose, one apple slice for the mouth, a banana slice for each ear and three carrot sticks for the hair.

17

Let the children dig in! Serve with cold water or juice.

DEVOTIONS

Many aspects about the story of Jesus' death and resurrection concern the numbers one, two, or three. Use this to help share the crucifixion story, pointing out any things that relate to these numbers. Open the Bible to John 17-20 so the children can associate the story with the Bible:

One night Jesus took His friends to a garden to pray. Jesus knew that it was time for Him to die, and He felt all alone. He prayed to God, His Father.

Afterward a man named Judas led the soldiers to Jesus. They took Jesus away to kill Him, even though He had not done anything bad. God's Son took the punishment for the bad things we may do, because He loves us.

The soldiers took Jesus to a hill where they put three crosses. Jesus was in the center between two other men. His friends were very sad because He died, but they wouldn't be sad for long.

After being dead for three days, Jesus came back to life. One woman named Mary Magdalene saw that Jesus' tomb was empty, so she went and told two of Jesus' friends, Peter and John. Later Jesus came and talked to Mary, and she knew it was really true that He was alive again. All of Jesus' friends were happy again.

Our Bible verse for today reminds us of the very special message that Jesus died for us and then came back to life: "God. . . loved us, and sent His Son" (I John 4:10). **Let's say the verse together.**

Sing "Jesus Loves Me" with the children. Pray in closing, thanking God for sending His Son Jesus because He loved us so much.

INVITATION

Count on coming to the

1-2-3 Group

DATE   TIME   PLACE

CERTIFICATE FOR DUPLICATION

YOU CAN COUNT ON JESUS!

Student's Name

was an important member of the 1-2-3 Group

at

Church Name

Date

Group Leader's Name

Animals and Rainbows

Memory Verse: "I have set My rainbow in the clouds."
Genesis 9:13 (NIV)

IDEA What two things could fill a child with wonder as much as animals and rainbows? This theme provides fun learning activities to help your students discover that Noah trusted in God, and the Lord gave him a promise.

PUBLICITY

After filling in the details on the invitation pattern, duplicate enough for all the children.

Enlarge the pattern to use as a poster, decorating it with magazine pictures of various animals. Use brightly-colored markers to fill in the lettering.

DECORATIONS & PREPARATION

Make several copies of the page of animal patterns. Cover a wall with rolled paper as a background for a long row of animals standing in pairs ready to enter the ark (you may use a pair of animals more than once).

Use extra copies to decorate the rest of the room. For instance, stand a few animals on the refreshment table or tape some to the chalkboard.

Make a rainbow by taping various colors of crepe paper in an arc beginning at one wall, going up to the ceiling, and coming down again across the room to that wall.

ACTIVITIES

What Is It Like in the Ark?
What you'll need: Animal mural (see Preparation)

You may want to help the children name the animals on the wall. Then point to each picture individually and ask the children to act out how this animal sounds and how it moves. The children will enjoy becoming a room full of hungry lions or tall giraffes.

Color the Rainbow
What you'll need: Rainbow pattern, variety of fruit, paper sack, and crayons

Draw a simple rainbow on an 8 ½ by 11 inch sheet of paper and duplicate one pattern for each guest expected. Color a rainbow ahead of time as an example for the children to follow.

Put several pieces of fruit in a paper bag; the colors should match the colors on your rainbow (e.g. banana/yellow). Ask the children, **Can you match a fruit with a color in the rainbow?** Point to each color and ask the students if they know what the color is. Show the children how the color matches the area of the rainbow that you have colored. Let the children scribble color their rainbow pictures.

Creative Clay
What you'll need: Peanut butter, honey, powdered milk, animal cookie cutters, paper plates, a pen, and plastic wrap

Be sure the children wash their hands with soap and water prior to helping you make the creative clay and be prepared to spend time helping the children clean up after this activity.

Mix together 1 cup peanut butter, 1 cup honey and 2 cups powdered milk. You may want to double the recipe depending on the number of students you have.

Display a variety of plastic animal cookie cutters and ask the children to name the animals. Then give each child a portion of the modeling clay and let him choose a cookie cutter. You and your helpers may need to help the children apply enough pressure to cut through the modeling clay. Put their creative animals on paper plates for the snack.

REFRESHMENTS

Have the children line up two by two for their creative clay animal snacks. Peel and cut up the fruit from the previous activity for the children to share as well. Serve with water or juice.

DEVOTIONS

Genesis 6:9-9:17 relates the story of the righteous man Noah and the lesson he learned of faith and obedience. Help your students understand this lesson. Open your Bible to the passage so the children associate the story with the Bible:

God was sad because people were disobeying Him. Only one man, Noah, and his family chose to be friends with God and listen to Him.

One day God told Noah to build a big boat called an ark. God was going to send lots of rain to the earth, so Noah needed to gather together all the animals to keep them safe.

Noah obeyed God. He built the ark and put all the animals inside, along with his family. Then the big storm came and it rained and rained.

Would you have been afraid if you had been Noah? Do you think Noah trusted God to help him?

God did take care of Noah and Noah remembered to offer thanks to God. Then God gave Noah a very special promise in the sky. Do you know what it is? God put a beautiful rainbow in the sky, just like the one we colored today. The rainbow is God's special promise that He will never let it rain that hard and long again.

God told Noah, "I have set My rainbow in the clouds" (Genesis 9:13, NIV). Let's say that verse together.

If you have time, enlist the aid of your helpers to write the verse on the children's papers. Repeat the verse several times with the students and close in a brief prayer thanking God for His promise.

INVITATION

PATTERNS FOR DUPLICATION

Ages 4 & 5

King for a Day	24
Irish Smilin' Time	27
Dannylions	30
Creature Convention	34

King for a Day

Memory Verse: "The Lord is King for ever and ever."
Psalm 10:16

IDEA
Young children know that kings are important people, and that they usually live in wealth. Your students will enjoy this opportunity to pretend they are royalty, with all the rights and privileges! The students will also discover, though, that as children of God, we *are* royalty.

PUBLICITY
Fill in the details on the pattern and duplicate to make invitations. For a poster, enlarge the pattern and set it on a background of parchment paper rolled at the edges to look like a scroll.

DECORATIONS & PREPARATION
Use shiny gold crepe paper to hang streamers across the room and/or to make a "throne" for all the children by decorating their chairs.

Since purple is considered the royal color, try to find a purple tablecloth (a paper one will do fine) and use the gold crepe paper down the center.

Other than the opening craft activity, you will not need any other materials for this activity.

ACTIVITIES

King's Crown
What you'll need: Duplicated crown pattern, scissors, aluminum foil, tape, markers, and shiny star stickers

Duplicate the crown pattern onto construction paper or other heavy paper. Give a pattern to each child as he arrives and let him cut out the crown. Tape the ends of the strips to the corresponding edges of the crown. Help each child wrap a sheet of aluminum foil around the crown and tape it securely on the back. Use a marker to write his name on the foil, then let him place a half dozen or so star stickers around his name. Insert Flap A through Slit B so that the crown fits the child's head.

King Saul and David
What you'll need: Room to play

Seat the children in a circle. Select one child to be "King Saul" and have a helper take him just outside the room for a moment. The other players choose one in the circle to be "David," who will lead them in all sorts of physical actions, such as stamping, clapping, waving, shaking their heads, etc. Bring King Saul back into the center of the circle. As the circle players change from action to action, King Saul has three guesses to try to find David. If he succeeds, David becomes the new King Saul and leaves the room. The first King Saul joins the circle. If King Saul doesn't guess correctly, he goes out again, or choose another child to be King Saul.

Have You Seen the King?
What you'll need: Room to play

Have all the players seated in a circle and select one child to be "It." He should stand behind one of the children and, touching him on the head, ask the question, "Have you seen the king?" The child should answer, "I don't think so, but what is he wearing?" The first child should describe someone in the circle, saying something like, "He's wearing green and blue stripes and cowboy boots." That student, recognizing the description of himself, should get up and try to run around the circle and back to his spot before "It" tags him. If he is not tagged, he is safe and the runner is "It" again.

The King Says
What you'll need: Room to play

This is a variation of the familiar game "Simon Says." Preface your playing time with an explanation that the people of a country must listen to their king. Tell your students that they are to do what the pretend king in this game says, but only when he calls himself the king.

Select a child to be the "king," instructing him to say to the others, "The king says jump up in the air," and so on. You may have to help him know what kinds of directions to give. Occasionally he may use his own name, such as "Gary says to turn around," but the students are to follow what he says only when he gives directions as the king.

Since this game is a little more challenging for the youngsters, let them sit out just one round if they make a mistake. Choose a new king every few rounds.

REFRESHMENTS

Serve a "kingly" feast of seedless grapes, cheese, and crackers on gold-colored paper plates and provide grape juice in clear plastic tumblers. If you think it would go over well, have the children pretend to be "His Royal Majesty's Food-Tasters." Pass out the refreshments to one child seated at the end of the table. He is to take one taste and "give his approval" before the next child gets his food and drink, and so on down the row until all the boys and girls have been served.

DEVOTIONS

Talk with the students about their activities for the day, asking them how it felt to pretend they were kings and queens.

Ask, **Did you know that in the Bible Jesus says He is a real king?** Read John 18:37, then discuss with the children what they think His kingdom is like. **Does it have lots of gold and jewels? Does Jesus sit on a big shiny throne?** Read John 18:36 to show that His kingdom is not like the ones here on earth. Jesus is a Ruler in God's heavenly kingdom, and Psalm 72:11 says that all the kings on earth will bow down to Him, because He is the King over all the other kings. And Jesus won't be King for just a day—Daniel 4:3 says His kingdom will last forever. Ask the children to repeat the memory verse with you.

Tell the children about the really good news, that we can be a part of God's kingdom. Read Matthew 25:34 and talk about how we can be "joint heirs" with Jesus when we show God our love for Him. Close with prayer.

INVITATION

Hear Ye! Hear Ye! Come and be a King for a Day

DATE:
TIME:
PLACE:

PATTERNS FOR DUPLICATION

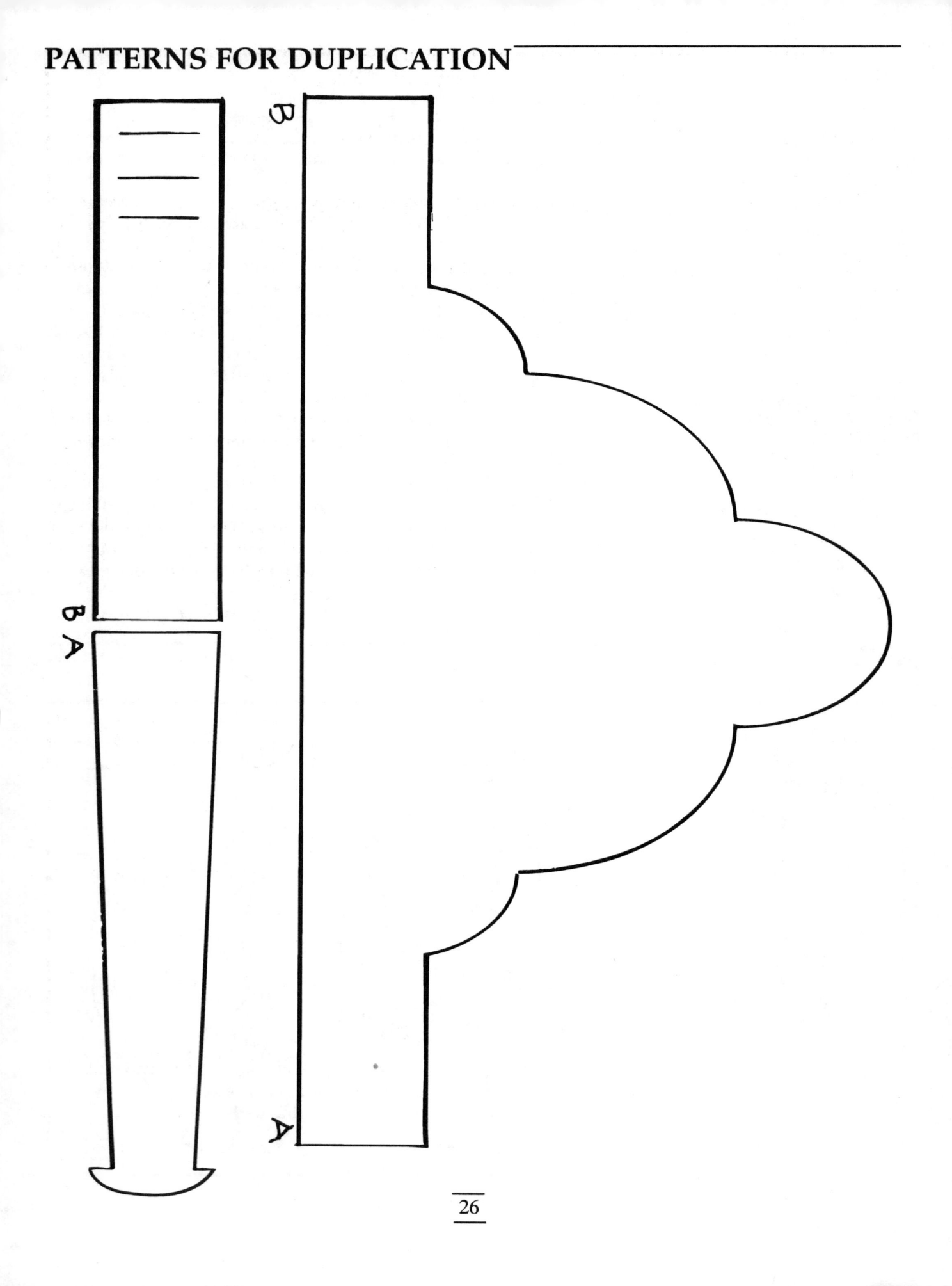

Irish Smilin' Time

Memory Verse: "There are three that bear record in heaven... and these three are one." I John 5:7

IDEA
The traditions of Ireland and St. Patrick's Day make it easy to put this party together in a way that your young students will enjoy. And like St. Patrick himself, you can use the shamrock to help the children see that God is Three in One.

PUBLICITY

Write down the title and details on the shamrock pattern and duplicate onto green paper to make invitations. Duplicate the poster (enlarging if you wish) and brighten it up by cutting various colors of construction paper to fit in the rainbow.

Since you will be using gold coin chocolates as prizes, sample one yourself so you can use the wrapper for the poster! Crumple the gold foil and glue at the top of the pot to represent the "pot 'o gold."

DECORATIONS & PREPARATION

Get out the green! Duplicate the shamrock pattern as many times as you wish and hang these around the room, either on the walls or from the ceiling.

If you feel really ambitious, make a rainbow out of 9 by 12 inch construction paper and use a black kettle at the "rainbow's end." The kettle can hold the green punch at refreshment time.

ACTIVITIES

Shamrock Cookie Cutting

What you'll need: Sugar cookie dough, waxed paper, green candy sprinkles, toothpick, baking sheets, and access to an oven

Prepare the cookie dough ahead of time and refrigerate until needed (see recipe at right). As a helper takes the children to wash their hands, set up a sheet of waxed paper on a work table for each student. Put enough dough onto the waxed paper for the child to make three two-inch circles, plus a little extra.

When the boys and girls return, show them how to take some dough and roll it into a ball, then flatten it to make a circle; they should do the same with two more pieces of dough. Help them form a shamrock by overlapping the three circles and gently "mashing" them together. Next the students should take the last bit of cookie dough, roll it into a stick, flatten it to make a stem, and attach it to the shamrock.

Let each child add some green sprinkles to his cookie. Use the toothpick to prick his initials into the stem (making sure the pricks are large enough that they will not bake out). At this point the children's roles in making the cookies will be done, so have your helper take them to get their hands washed again. (Rolling the dough will make hands rather slimy, so be careful that they do not touch anything along the way!)

Carefully peel the formed cookie dough off the waxed paper and place onto the baking sheets. Bake according to the directions.

Easy Sugar Cookies
1 ½ cups Bisquick
2 packages instant vanilla* pudding mix
½ cup vegetable oil
2 eggs

* If desired, pistachio pudding mix could be used so that cookies are green, or add a few drops of green food coloring to the vanilla mix.

27

Preheat oven to 350 degrees. Mix all the ingredients together until the dough forms a ball. Shape into balls and flatten according to directions given above. Bake on an ungreased baking sheet for eight minutes. Do not overbake.

This recipe makes enough for about ten children to make shamrock cookies. Double or halve the recipe to make the right amount for your group.

Pot 'O Gold
What you'll need: Two bags of gold foil-wrapped chocolates and two coin banks

Divide the group into two teams and have them line up in single file. Make sure the bags have an equal number of chocolates.

On your signal the first children in each line will begin taking gold coins out of their bags and passing them to the next students. The boys and girls should continue passing the chocolates, one at a time, to their neighbors until they reach the last student, who drops the coins into a bank on the floor.

The first team to have all its coins in its bank wins. Both teams may eat the chocolates, but let the winning team have its share first.

Hot Potato
What you'll need: Two large russet potatoes and two circles of chairs

Before you play this traditional game with the children, explain to them that potatoes are one of the main crops in Ireland, which is where St. Patrick's Day started.

Group the children into one of the circles. Set a timer to go off in thirty seconds and have the students start passing the "hot" potato as quickly as they can. When the alarm rings, the student holding the potato leaves the first circle and goes into the second circle. As more children enter the second circle, start a game there as well. Let the students continue going back and forth.

If you wish, award everyone a small prize, such as coupons for free food. Call a restaurant and ask about these—many times managers will give away coupons for promotional purposes.

REFRESHMENTS

It should be no surprise that the children will eat their own cookies for refreshments! If you want to give them an extra treat, serve the cookies

INVITATION

with mint chocolate chip or pistachio ice cream. Provide milk or lemon-lime punch prepared with Kool-aid and soda to drink.

DEVOTIONS

What you'll need: A shamrock from the decorations and a marking pen.

Use one of the shamrocks from the decorations as a visual aid to teach this Bible lesson.

Read to the children the story of Jesus' baptism found in Luke 3:21-22 (NIV).

Ask the children, **Did you notice who was there when Jesus was baptized?** (Jesus, of course, was there.) Hold up the shamrock and point to one of the side leaflets. Say, **We can say that this leaf stands for Jesus.** Use a big marker to write "Jesus" on the leaflet.

Next point out the first part of verse 22, which speaks of the Holy Spirit coming like a dove. Point to the opposite leaflet and tell the students that we can let it represent the Holy Spirit. Write "Holy Spirit" on the leaflet.

Read the last part of verse 22 again and say, **The voice from heaven said Jesus was His Son. Who is Jesus' Father? That's right, God is His Father.** Write "Father" in the top leaflet.

Ask the children to repeat the names of the Deity represented on the shamrock. Say, **Each part of the shamrock is important, isn't it, or else it wouldn't be a whole shamrock? The Bible shows us that God is like this shamrock, because He is all three in one—the Holy Spirit, Jesus, and the Father.** Write "3 in 1" on the back side of the shamrock, then say the memory verse with the students.

Sing with the children the following song to the tune of "Frere Jacques," pointing to the appropriate leaflets on the shamrock as you sing:

God the Father, God the Father,
God the Son, God the Son,
God the Holy Spirit, God the Holy Spirit,
Three in One, Three in One.

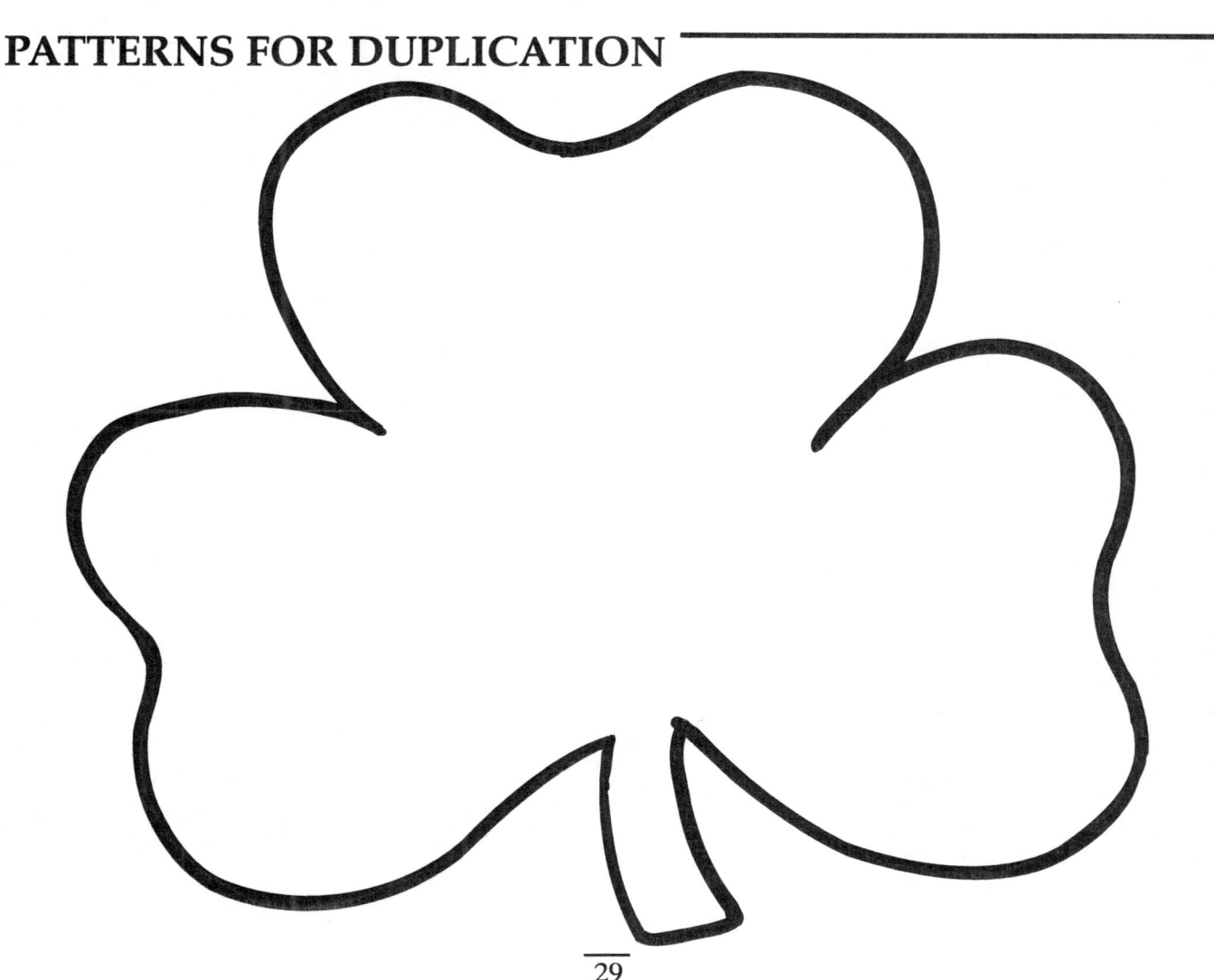

PATTERNS FOR DUPLICATION

Dannylions

Memory Verse: "My heart trusts in Him, and I am helped."
Psalm 28:7 (NIV)

IDEA
Centered around the Bible story of Daniel in the lions' den, this plan will provide fun while the children learn how God protects those who trust in Him. The theme will also help the students recognize the colors yellow and orange.

PUBLICITY
Fill in the details on the invitation and duplicate. If desired, enlarge the pattern and decorate with yellow and orange yarn.

DECORATIONS & PREPARATION
Now is the time to put those dandelions in your yard to good use—by using them to decorate the room!

Gather a few dandelions and place in vases to use as centerpieces for the serving tables. If you have orange flowers available, such as marigolds or poppies, use those as well.

Depending on the quantity of flowers and the time available, make garlands to hang in various places around the room. With sturdy string, tie the dandelions in a long row close to the blossoms. Keep the garlands fresh until use by carefully placing them in water.

Tape down a white paper tablecloth or long sheet of poster paper onto the working tables the children will be using. In front of each student's seat, tape down the lion pattern (page 46) onto the tablecloth.

Duplicate one lion's tail end for each student. For the game, enlarge the lion pattern.

ACTIVITIES

Colorful Lions
What you'll need: Table prepared with covering (see Preparation) and crayons

The children will feel included in the preparation of this meeting by being able to decorate the tablecloth. Let each child color the pattern in front of him.

Lion's Tail
What you'll need: Duplicated pattern for tail end, crayons, 8 inch piece of yellow yarn, and tape

Write each child's name on the back of his lion's tail—he will use it in later games. Let the children color their tails with crayons and tape to one end of the yarn.

Daniel in the Lions' Den
What you'll need: Lions' tails

Have the children stand in a large circle holding the tails they made behind them. They will pretend to be the lions. One child should stand in the center of the circle—he or she will play Daniel. The lions will start the game by walking around Daniel in a circle singing the following song to the tune of "Here We Go 'Round the Mulberry Bush:"

Lions: *(moving in a circle around Daniel)*
  Daniel in the lions' den, lions' den, lions' den,
  Daniel in the lions' den, oh what is he to do?
Lions: *(Daniel kneels down and folds his hands as if in prayer)*
  Pray to the Lord and He'll save you, He'll save you, He'll save you;
  Pray to the Lord and He'll save you. That's what you've got to do!
Daniel and Teacher: *(The lions stop moving and one by one squat down and cover their mouths)*
  He prayed and the lions' mouths were shut,

mouths were shut, mouths were shut;
He prayed and the lions' mouths were shut

Everyone: *(Lions jump up with arms in the air!)*
Daniel, God saved you!

Repeat the game several times, having the children take turns playing Daniel.

Pin the Tail on the Lion
What you'll need: Duplicated lion pattern, lions' tails, masking tape, and blindfold

Secure the lion pattern at the children's level to a wall or board. Put a roll of masking tape on the backs of the children's lion tails at the end of the yarn. Let the students take turns trying to place their lions' tails in the proper position on the lion. If a child does not want to use the blindfold, he may simply close his eyes. Turning the child around is not necessary.

The child who places his lion's tail closest to the proper position wins! Award a small prize, such as a bag of orange and yellow candy corn.

REFRESHMENTS

Ask the children to name different foods that are yellow or orange. Provide some of these foods, either individually or as a "smorgasbord" of tastes. Some suggested foods would be chips, cheese puffs, cheese slices, carrot sticks, lemon cookie bars, bananas, and orange slices; drinks could be lemonade, orange drink, or juice.

DEVOTIONS

Open your Bible to Daniel 6:10-23, which relates the story of Daniel's faithfulness and trust in God. Tell the children that many of the men who worked for the king didn't like Daniel, even though the king liked him. The men tricked the king into writing a law that could not be changed. Daniel prayed to God even though this new law said he could not.

Ask the children, **What happened to Daniel because he did not obey the law?** (He was thrown into the lions' den.) Explain that even though the lions were probably going to kill him, Daniel trusted in God. Ask, **What did God do?** (He loved Daniel so much that He sent an angel to shut the lions' mouths. The lions could not hurt him.) **This tells us that when we trust in God, He will protect us.**

Say the memory verse with the children, then close with prayer, thanking God for His protection.

INVITATION

PATTERNS FOR DUPLICATION

PATTERNS FOR DUPLICATION

Creature Convention

Memory Verse: "He hath made every thing beautiful in His time." Ecclesiastes 3:11

IDEA
Colorful butterflies emerging from hard, brown cocoons; fireflies glowing in the night; bees transforming pollen into sweet, sticky honey—children are fascinated by bugs and "beasties." Use this attraction to insects as an opportunity to familiarize children with the small wonders of God's big world.

PUBLICITY
Using a heavy dark marker, print the information on the invitation pattern. Duplicate the pattern onto red paper at normal size to make invitations and at a larger size to make a poster.

DECORATIONS & PREPARATION
Cut pictures from outdoors or scientific types of magazines to make a collage of bugs familiar to fours and fives—bees, butterflies, ladybugs, grasshoppers, worms, fireflies, etc. Glue the pictures to poster board and hang the finished collage by the entrance to the room.

The children will be making the rest of the decorations, so make sure you hold the activity where you will have space for a craft area and for the relay activities.

Devotions will be extra meaningful if you can have some real live bugs for the children to see! Ask the junior class teacher for help from her students in finding a collection of various harmless insects, such as ladybugs, grasshoppers, sow bugs (the little gray ones that roll up into a ball), and so on. Caterpillars and butterflies will be a part of the Bible lesson, so you will especially want to try to have the juniors find these.

Instruct the juniors to bring the bugs to you in see-through jars with grass, leaves, and twigs in them. Make sure you emphasize that the lids should have holes poked in them so that the insects have air.

ACTIVITIES

Butterflies Flutter By
What you'll need: Wing pattern duplicated onto colorful construction paper, scissors, crayons, 1 by 8 ½ inch black paper strips with rounded ends, 2 inch lengths of black chenille wire, tape, glue, and string

Let the children cut out the wing patterns using the colors of their choice. Help them put the butterfly together by inverting the wings so that the pointed ends overlap about 1 inch (see diagram); tape together. Let the children color their butterflies, then glue the black strip over the center to make the body and glue the chenille wires at one end for the antennae.

Write the children's names on the back as they finish. Tape a length of string to the back and hang the butterflies from the ceiling.

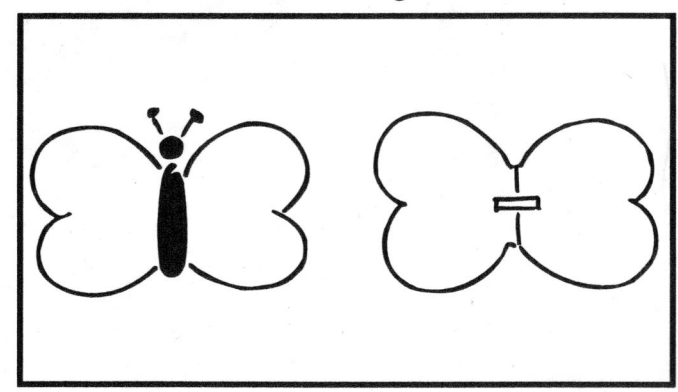

Creeping Crawlies
What you'll need: Room to play

Divide the group into two teams and have them stand behind a starting line. Select one child to stand 20 feet away and hold out his arms like a tree. On your signal the first children in each line will

34

begin crawling on all fours toward the "tree," then turn around and come back. The next ones in line may go when the first ones return. The first team to complete the relay wins. Award small prizes such as gummy worms. For a second round have the children "fly" to the tree by flapping their "wings."

REFRESHMENTS

Spread graham crackers with peanut butter and a few drops of honey (to avoid dripping). Serve with cups of cold milk.

DEVOTIONS

What you'll need: Insects collected by the older children (see Preparation)

You will want to keep the insects out of sight and out of reach until you are ready for this segment. Make sure you have enough helpers so the jars can be placed on several tables and so the children have room to move freely. Let the boys and girls get up close to watch the bugs.

Talk about the insects' features and how they function—little feet that carry them all over the plants, antennae to help them observe what is going on, etc. If you feel it is appropriate, you might let the students take turns holding a ladybug or other insect. Make sure little hands are washed before you continue.

If you have a caterpillar in one of the jars, direct the children's attention to it. Note how it looks like a dark, fuzzy worm. Next point to a butterfly, whether real or one of the paper ones hanging from the ceiling. Tell the children that one of the wonders about the world God made is that caterpillars turn into butterflies when they grow up.

Ask the students to say the memory verse with you, then talk about how people can become new creatures too. Read II Corinthians 5:17 and say, **When we become new creatures, we don't turn into pretty butterflies, but we become beautiful on the inside. Jesus Christ, Who is God's Son, makes us new and beautiful when we show our love for Him.**

Close with a prayer that helps the children focus on loving God, thus finding out what it means to be a new creature in Christ.

INVITATION

COME BE A PART OF THE
CREATURE
CONVENTION!!

DATE TIME
PLACE

PATTERNS FOR DUPLICATION

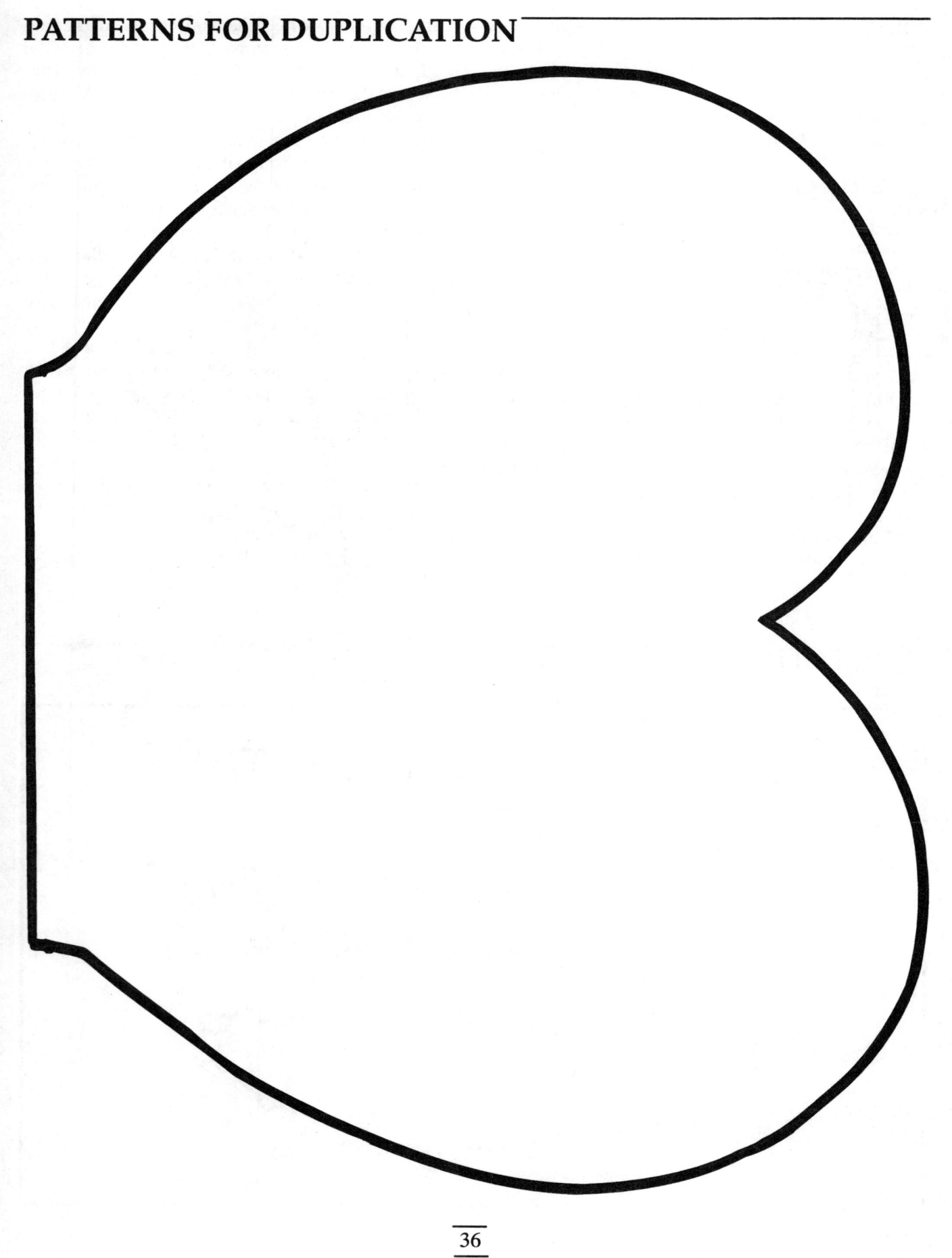

Grades 1 & 2

Joyful Jubilee 38
April Showers 41
Backward Bash 44
May Play Day 47

Joyful Jubilee

Memory Verse: "Make a joyful noise unto the Lord, all the earth: make a loud noise, and rejoice, and sing praise." Psalm 98:4

IDEA

As you have watched your students at play you have probably noticed that many of them make up tunes as well as sing the songs that they have learned at school, church, home and from their friends. As the Bible calls them to, the boys and girls will really have fun making a "joyful noise unto the Lord."

PUBLICITY

After filling in the specifics on the pattern, duplicate at normal size for invitations and enlarge to make a poster.

During class time, ask three or four students to help you publicize the jubilee by leading the others in song. Provide them with a few samples of the instruments they will be making at the party. Have the helpers stand in front and play the instruments while the entire group sings a familiar song. Verbally announce the event after the song is over.

DECORATIONS & PREPARATION

Decorations could include pictures of musical instruments cut from magazines and musical notes cut from construction paper. Decorate the refreshment table with toy instruments or the sample instruments used for the publicity.

You will need help from the parents or other members of your congregation in gathering some of the supplies for the "Instrument Shop." Set up equipment tables and work areas so each guest can make a paper plate shaker and/or a drum.

Invite at least one person to the party who proficiently plays a melody instrument, such as a piano, accordion, or harmonica. Work with him on planning the singing time for devotions; at meeting time provide a list of the songs to be sung.

ACTIVITIES

The Instrument Shop

Help the boys and girls with the following directions. Remember to provide scissors, tape, crayons, and glue at the work tables.

Drum

Take a round oatmeal box and secure the lid, or a substitute lid made of a couple pieces of heavy construction paper, with tape. Add a string so the drum can be hung around the neck, then cover it with construction paper and stickers. Use pencils for drumsticks.

Paper Plate Shaker

Decorate the bottom sides of two paper plates with crayons, fabric scraps, stickers, etc. Put beans, pebbles or marbles between the plates (front sides facing each other). With a hole punch make holes in the edges of the plates and sew the plates together with yarn. Make a yarn handle.

Rhythmical Chairs

What you'll need: Circle of chairs and the children's hand-made instruments

Set up chairs in the same manner as for musical chairs with one less chair than players. Have the students circle around the chairs, each one holding his drum or paper plate shaker. One person should start a rhythm with his instrument and the others should copy it. The students will march around the chairs, playing the rhythm until you say "stop." Then everyone will scramble to sit in a chair.

The student who does not get a chair is out, but he can still participate from the sidelines by using his rhythm instrument. "Out" players can take turns starting a rhythm. Keep removing a chair each round until only one person remains.

Performer's Platform
What you'll need: Small rugs or mats, melody instrument or recorded music, and the children's rhythm instruments

Place several small rugs or mats around the room on the floor. You or the invited musician should play a melody instrument or some recorded music. Meanwhile, the children should march around the room keeping time to the music with their instruments and stepping on the mats when they come to them. When the music stops, they must freeze where they are. Everyone who has at least one foot on a mat is on the "performer's platform" and gets to stay for the next round. Everyone who is not on a "platform" leaves the game until the next round. Continue playing until the children are ready for another game.

REFRESHMENTS

Bake cupcakes and spread with white frosting. Add a chocolate kiss and some pieces of black licorice to make a musical note. Serve with punch.

DEVOTIONS

Sing songs that are the favorites of your group. The children can keep time to the rhythm with their instruments. Start with some familiar fun songs, then go on to some of the quieter songs.

The children are probably familiar with the story of David and Goliath (found in I Samuel 17), so ask them to each tell one thing about how the story happened. Point out that David faced both tough times and good times as he was growing up and when he became king of Israel. All throughout his life, though, David expressed his feelings to God with the help of music.

Ask the children, **Did you know that the psalms are actually the words for the songs David wrote? How many of us can say Psalm 23?** Say the chapter with all the children. Tell the boys and girls that David trusted in the Lord for His help and strength, and he made sure to praise and thank the Lord.

Read Psalm 98, emphasizing that the seas and the hills can "praise" the Lord. Repeat the memory verse, then ask the students what they can be joyful about. Close with a prayer of thanksgiving.

INVITATION

Come make a joyful noise at the Joyful Jubilee

DATE: TIME: PLACE:

CERTIFICATE FOR DUPLICATION

I MADE A JOYFUL NOISE
at the
JOYFUL JUBILEE

Student's Name

Group Leader's Name

Date

April Showers

Memory Verse: "Whenever... the rainbow appears in the clouds, I will remember."
Genesis 9:14-15 (NIV)

IDEA

What can be more fun for children than to stomp through a puddle, laughing in the rain? This party captures the frolicsome fun of an April shower while also teaching some truths about that first rainfall, the story of Noah and the Flood.

PUBLICITY

Fill in the details on the pattern and duplicate for invitations.

Make a poster mobile by first enlarging the invitation pattern and then cutting out the individual raindrops. Suspend the drops from pieces of yarn tied to the framework of an umbrella and stand the umbrella where the children can see it.

DECORATIONS & PREPARATION

Borrow several umbrellas to stand around the room, saving one for the serving table. Duplicate the raindrop pattern onto colorful construction paper. The number you need will depend on the size of your group; you will need one of *any* color to give to each child expected and at least one of *every* color to put in a container. Cut just one red raindrop and put it with those in the container. Make a few extra raindrops to suspend from the ceiling with yarn or string as decoration.

Hold an umbrella and wear a raincoat as you greet the guests.

ACTIVITIES

Umbrella-Ball Toss
What you'll need: An umbrella, ping pong balls, and bag of chocolate kisses

Turn an umbrella upside down and place it about ten feet away from a designated line. Allow each child a turn in tossing five or six ping pong balls into the umbrella. Award one chocolate kiss for each ball that goes in.

Puddle Plop
What you'll need: Small juice glass, large pail, water, and pennies (Both old for game and new for prizes)

This game is best played outdoors or on a floor that can be easily wiped up.

Set the small juice glass in the bottom of the pail, then fill the pail with water enough to cover the glass a few inches. The object is for the children to plop pennies in the pail (use three to five), trying to get them to land in the glass. Divide the group into teams or play individually. Give shiny new pennies for prizes (one for each penny that landed in the glass).

Frozen Rain Relay
What you'll need: Four pans, ice cubes, and big serving spoons

Divide the group into two teams; the players will stand in two lines side by side. Set a pan at both ends of each team; fill two of the pans with ice. The first players take an ice cube with a spoon and pass them on to the next players in line. When the spoon and ice reach the last players, they dump the ice in the empty pan, go to the beginning of the line, take another ice cube on the spoon and pass it along. Play continues until all players are back in their original places. Award springtime stickers to the winning team.

Colored Raindrops Game
What you'll need: Duplicated raindrops in a container (See Preparation) and a circle of chairs

Seat all the children in a circle of chairs, except for one who will stand in the center. Reach into the container and pull out one colored raindrop. Everyone with that color must change seats, and the child in the center tries to get a seat in the ensuing scramble. The one left without a seat goes to the center for the next round. When the red raindrop is pulled out, *everyone* must change seats.

REFRESHMENTS

Cupcakes, each with a miniature paper or plastic umbrella stuck in the frosting, will be fun for the children. Serve the cupcakes with lemonade or punch.

DEVOTIONS

The children may hold their raindrops left over from the Colored Raindrop Game as you begin the devotional time. Have them look at their raindrops while you tell them that a long time ago, back near the time when God first made the world, people didn't know what raindrops were because they had never seen them. Then God sent the big rainstorm that lasted for 40 days and 40 nights, and the water flooded the earth. Ask the students if any of them know who was a part of that story (Noah).

Turn to Genesis 6-9 for the account of the Flood. Tell the story of how the Lord was saddened by how wicked the people were, so He decided to wipe mankind from the face of the earth. Only one man, Noah, and his family would be saved.

Say, **After Noah did as God instructed by building the ark and bringing in all the animals two by two, God shut the door of the big boat. Then the rains came, and it poured and poured for days on end. When the land was dry again, Noah and his family stepped out of the ark. God made a promise that He would never again destroy the earth with a flood, and across the sky He set a big, beautiful rainbow as a sign of His promise.**

Following the Bible lesson, set out a container of crayons and let the children draw rainbows on the backs of their raindrops. On the front they may write something to help remind them of the Lord's promise: "God says, 'I will remember.'"

End the get-together with prayer, thanking God for rain and for His promise.

INVITATION

PATTERNS FOR DUPLICATION

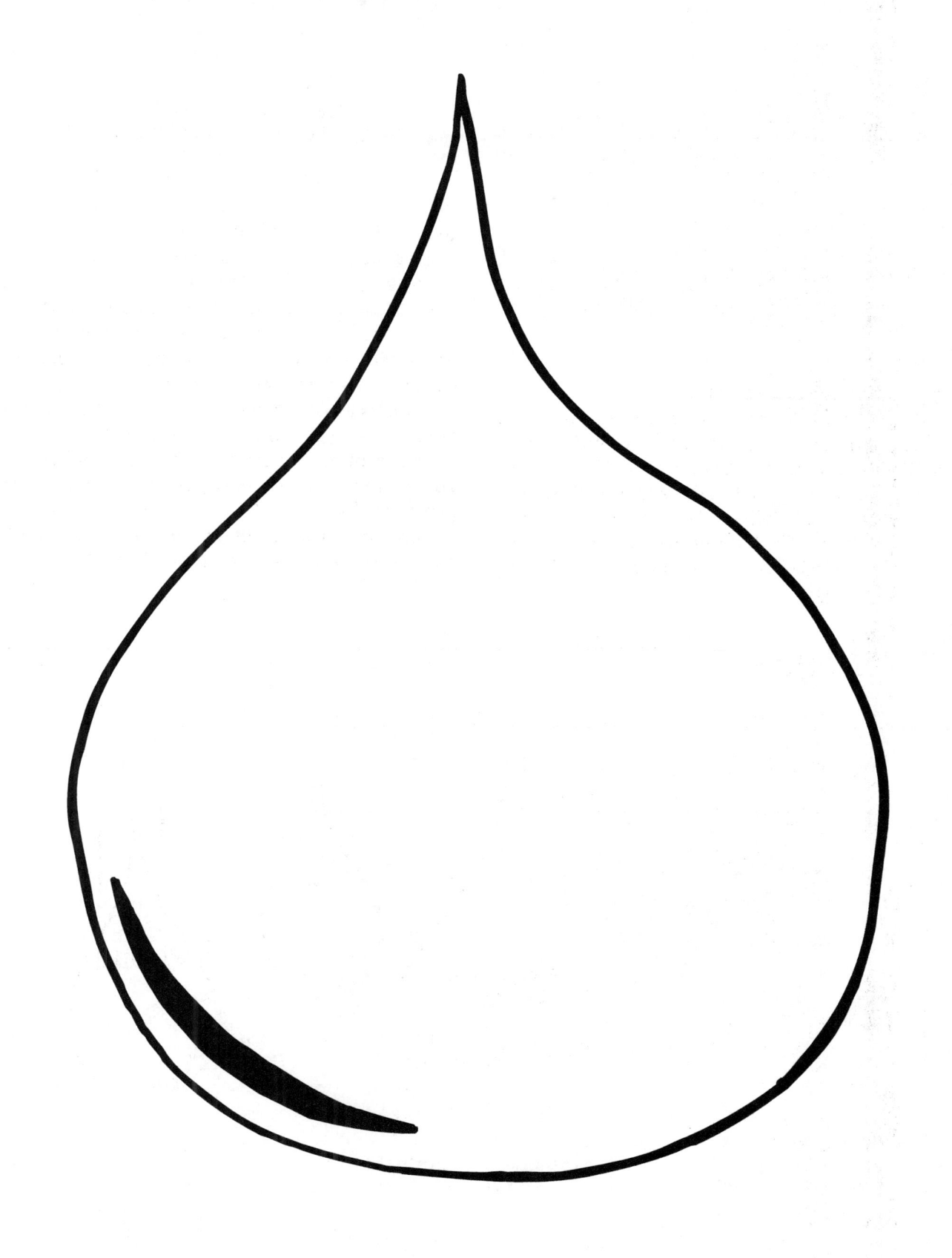

Backward Bash

Memory Verse: "Follow my example, as I follow the example of Christ." I Corinthians 11:1 (NIV)

IDEA
This meeting has all the elements of the others, but with a terrific twist that will make for some silly fun from the first "goodbye" to the last "hello." Along with the backward thrust will be the lesson to focus straight ahead on our leader, Jesus.

PUBLICITY
After filling in the details, duplicate the pattern for invitations and enlarge for posters.

If you like, develop a skit for the class featuring a couple of helpers with their clothes on backward. Have them come into the meeting room and greet each other with "goodbye," talk about the bash and part with "hello."

DECORATIONS & PREPARATION
Prepare the room the opposite from usual. In other words, place the chairs in a circle facing outward instead of in—or facing the wall. If you use any kind of decorations, make sure they are placed backwards!

Remind everyone to enter the room backward and greet the guests with "goodbye." Since the devotional time usually takes place at the end of a get-together, you'll want to include it at the *beginning* this time. Have the refreshments next, then go on to the activities. Be sure to say "Hello" as your guests leave!

ACTIVITIES

Lifesaver Relay
What you'll need: Toothpicks and Lifesaver® candy
Divide the group into teams and line them up vertically. Give each person a toothpick and give a piece of Lifesaver® candy as well to the student at the back of the line. This student must walk backward to a turn-around point and then return without dropping the Lifesaver. Then he will pass it directly onto the toothpick of the next person in line, who will repeat the action. If a toothpick or the Lifesaver is dropped, the player must start over. The first team to finish wins.

Crab Walk
What you'll need: Room to play
Line everyone up at a goal line on their hands and knees. Everyone must race toward the opposite goal backward, or sideways, crab-fashion.

Race in Reverse
What you'll need: Room to play
Starting from a wall and stretching as far as possible, the students will take five paces backward. The winner is the student who travels the farthest.

Turn-Around Toss
What you'll need: Beanbags
Line up the contestants a few at a time, side by side, and give each a beanbag. Without looking over his shoulders each one is to throw his beanbag backward as far as he can. Continue with new groups of players if you like, ending with a grand championship throw.

Backward Best-Dressed
What you'll need: Prizes
Award prizes to the best-dressed at the party—they should of course have their clothes on backward! If any children arrive with their clothes on in normal fashion, you can help them participate by turning a shirt backwards but make sure they are willing.

Have your helpers judge how the guests are dressed and decide who should win first, second, and third place. Let all the other students "win" too by naming them as honorable mentions. Award small prizes to everyone, such as erasers, fancy pencils, plastic puzzles, etc.

REFRESHMENTS

To be really backward, serve the dessert first, followed by the main course and then appetizers. Use a simple menu, such as pudding, soup and half-sandwiches, and carrot sticks. Remember something to drink, too—punch or hot chocolate.

DEVOTIONS

(Begin devotions as soon as you believe all the guests have arrived. Read through the following narrative so that you can relate it to the children with some familiarity:)

A lady named Jean Craighead George wrote a book called *Julie of the Wolves*. The author spent time in the arctic land watching the habits of wolf packs. She found that the very largest wolf was usually the leader of the pack.

As the writer watched the wolves through her binoculars, she would often see this leader wolf stop and look around at the others. Then the rest of the pack would gather around the leader and nuzzle him under his chin as if to say, "You are still our leader. We are still following you. You are in charge." As big and powerful as he was, the leader needed to be reassured that the others were still following him.

Just as a runner in a race must keep his eyes on the goal, so we should keep our eyes on Jesus. We do not need to look behind us for approval. What might happen if we are looking backward, worrying about what others think? (We might trip or get lost from the path.)

If we love Jesus, we will want to follow His example. Then we can be sure that others who may be watching *our* lives will find that we are a good example of a follower of Christ.

In his first letter to the Corinthians, Paul told his Christian friends to follow the leader. Do you know who that leader was? It was Jesus Christ. Paul said in I Corinthians 11:1 (NIV), "Follow my example, as I follow the example of Christ."

That's a good goal for each of us to have. Let's pray together to follow the leader, Jesus Christ.

(If you wish, end the devotional time with the song, "I Have Decided To Follow Jesus.")

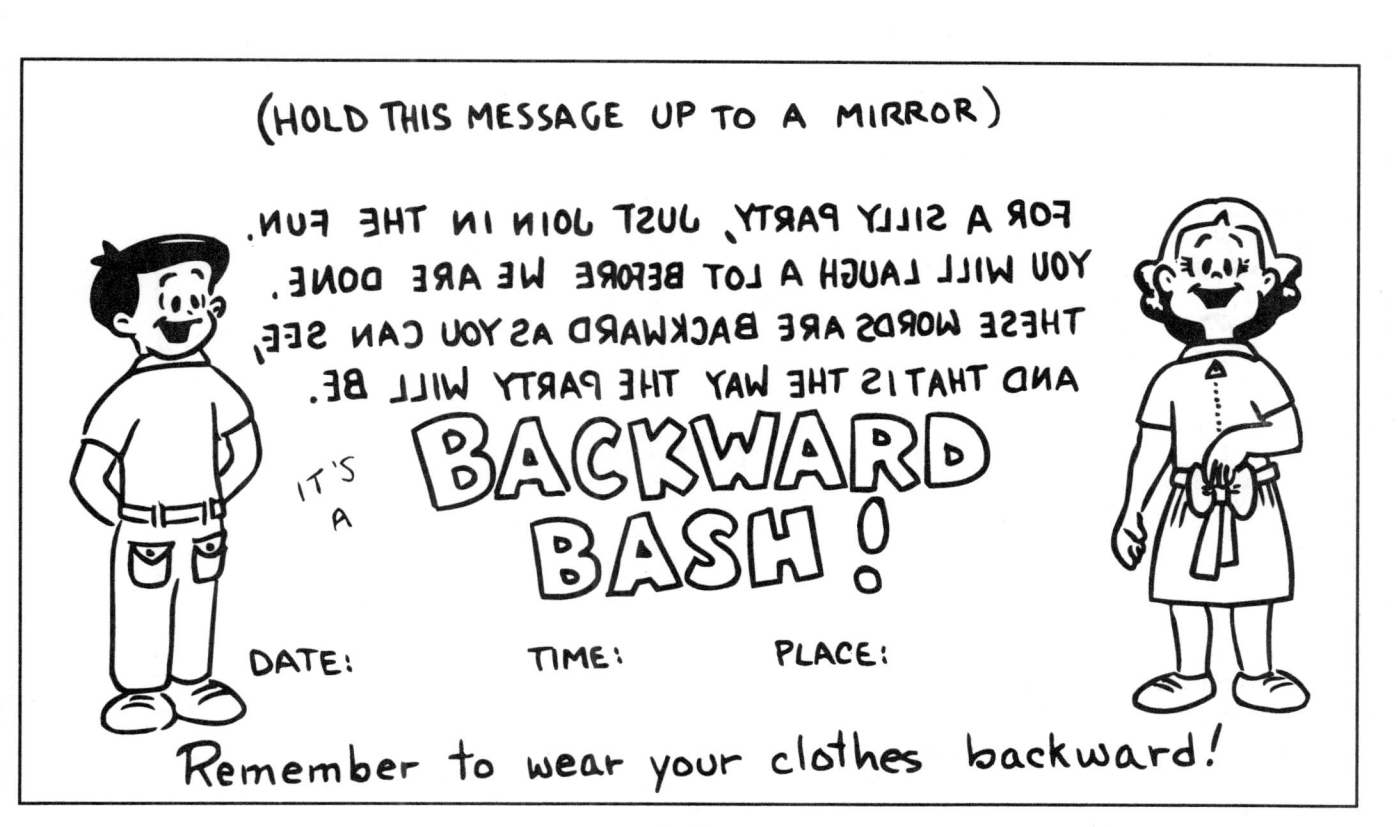

INVITATION

(HOLD THIS MESSAGE UP TO A MIRROR)

FOR A SILLY PARTY, JUST JOIN IN THE FUN.
YOU WILL LAUGH A LOT BEFORE WE ARE DONE.
THESE WORDS ARE BACKWARD AS YOU CAN SEE,
AND THAT IS THE WAY THE PARTY WILL BE.

IT'S A **BACKWARD BASH!**

DATE: TIME: PLACE:

Remember to wear your clothes backward!

CERTIFICATE FOR DUPLICATION

JESUS SETS US STRAIGHT!

Student's Name

was a star of the Backward Bash

at

Church Name

Group Leader's Name

Date

May Play Day

Memory Verse: "The flower fadeth: but the word of our God shall stand for ever." Isaiah 40:8

IDEA
This special time celebrates the arrival of May with a variety of fun, flower-filled games. The children will come to understand that, although beauty is fleeting, the truth of God's Word will always be with us.

PUBLICITY
Fill in the details on the invitation pattern, then duplicate onto colorful paper. Enlarge the pattern to make a poster. Staple plastic spring flowers around the edges to make a border.

DECORATIONS & PREPARATION
The children will have great fun wrapping a Maypole and decorating it with flowers. Just have a wooden pole in place beforehand; a 2 by 2 inch piece of lumber will substitute well if you do not have a round broom pole. For the pole holder, a pail of sand or dirt will serve the purpose. If you are meeting in a basement, just use one of the support posts.

Help the boys and girls by tacking pink crepe paper streamers to the top. As the students arrive, they may wrap a streamer around the pole and tape it to the bottom with tape. Those who arrive later may tuck in flowers (real or plastic) here and there and secure with tape.

If your pole is portable, it might be a good idea to place it at one side of the room so as not to interfere with active games.

Make sure you have a flowery centerpiece for the serving table. If you wish, add extra decorations by cutting out pictures of flowers from magazines, or making some yourself with construction paper.

You will need a bouquet or arrangement of flowers (preferably with a variety) for the devotional. Try to have as many flowers as the number of children you expect at the meeting.

ACTIVITIES

May Basket Relay
What you'll need: Plastic or paper flowers, two baskets, and a bag of gumdrops

Divide the group into two or more teams of equal size and give each player a flower—plastic or paper. With the players behind a starting line, set up a basket about twenty feet away that the students will run toward to make a "flower arrangement."

At the signal, the first member of each team heads for his team's basket to drop in his flower. The next children in line may go after the first ones tag their hands. The winning team will be the one with its flower arrangement done first. These students may be the first of the whole group to share a bag of gumdrops.

Mayflower Circle
What you'll need: Circle of chairs

Seat the children in a circle with one youngster in the middle designated as "It." Ask the boys and girls to number off by fours. After all have counted, assign flower names. The *ones* are roses; the *twos* are lilies; the *threes* are daisies; the *fours* are poppies. (Print the names of these four flowers on a chalkboard or a large sheet of paper to help the children remember what flower names to call out.)

When the child in the center calls one of the four flowers, everyone with that flower name must change places with someone who has the same flower name. For example, all the lilies exchange places, while the roses, poppies, and daisies remain seated. The child who is "It" will try to get a seat while the designated flowers are exchanging places. If he does, the one left without a place to sit becomes the new "It" and the one who was in the center becomes the same kind of flower that he caught. Occasionally, the child who is "It" can shout, "Flower basket upset!" Then *everyone* must find a different seat.

Watch the Birdie
What you'll need: A badminton shuttlecock

Have all the players but one stand in a circle. The remaining player stays inside the circle. The rest will throw a badminton shuttlecock to one another at random, being allowed to toss it from one side of the ring to the other. The player inside should attempt to intercept the birdie or run about, gently trying to take it out of the hands of the other players. If he succeeds, he should change places with the last player to touch or hold the birdie.

REFRESHMENTS

Make a variety of sandwiches. Cut each sandwich into triangles and place on a plate with the points turned inward and separated a little. Set a carrot, cut to about 2 inches high, top side up in the center of the sandwich shapes. Place a celery stick in between two of the triangle shapes. The sandwich is now in the shape of a flower! Add a few potato chips and serve with punch.

DEVOTIONS

To begin devotions, hold up an arrangement of live flowers for the children to see. Ask the boys and girls what things flowers need to help them grow (moist soil, water, sunlight, etc.). Encourage the students to notice the beauty of the flowers—the colors, shapes, fragrances, and so on. Say, **God made so many different flowers and they are all very beautiful. We should praise the Lord for making nature so pretty.**

Take a few moments to let the children offer sentence prayers of praise. When you resume the devotional, tell the children that even though the flowers are beautiful, someday they will shrivel up and wilt. Flowers are not made to last, but something far better is: the truth of the Bible.

Open the Scriptures and read Isaiah 40:8. Say, **Yes, flowers fade—even pretty May flowers—but God says His Word will always be true. His promise will last forever.** Repeat the Bible verse with the students, then give each child a flower from the arrangement to take home.

INVITATION

Come to the May Play Day

DATE: TIME: PLACE:

Grades 3 & 4

Frosty Fridge Time 50
Missions-Minded Progressive Dinner 53
Jolly Green Jubilee 56
Planting Project 59
Traffic Jam-Boree 62

Frosty "Fridge" Time

Memory Verse: *"Our help is in the name of the Lord, who made heaven and earth." Psalm 124:8*

IDEA

"Raiding" the refrigerator will be legal at this event! There will be an emphasis on the a-i-d, though, since part of the purpose is to aid in filling the pastor's pantry. In a practical way, the children will learn how helping is a way of serving the Lord.

PUBLICITY

If any classrooms have a child-size kitchen set, use the refrigerator as a part of your publicity. Place the refrigerator in the church foyer or any other place where the parents are sure to see it. Tape an announcement to the refrigerator asking the congregation to contribute food items for the pastor's family. Be sure to note that the food can be either refrigerated or dry goods.

Make regular invitations for your class. Duplicate the pattern after filling in the details of where and when to meet.

DECORATIONS & PREPARATION

Since the students will be bringing the food to the pastor as a part of the get-together, ask if he and his family would like to host the event at their home. Reassure them that you will take care of all the details!

If the pastor's family is open to having decorations, make arrangements to go over early with a few helpers. An easy way to decorate would be to make paper snowflakes. Fold circles or squares of white paper in half several times and cut various shapes along the folds. Unfold and place in several locations.

Read through the Refreshments to make sure you have all the necessary ingredients. Bring these to the pastor's house when you come over to do the decorations.

It might be fun to design a huge contemporary card that everyone may sign. A smiling refrigerator would be easy to draw, using a black marking pen on white poster board.

Set up a plan for transporting the children to the pastor's house. It would be a good idea to arrange for space in other refrigerators in case there is more food than your pastor's kitchen can handle.

ACTIVITIES

Refrigerator Raid

What you'll need: Donated food items and card signed by the congregation

The first order of the day will be to present the food to the pastor and his family. You can make this a meaningful presentation by involving the children; provide them opportunity to show their appreciation to the family if they so desire, and give the card at this time.

Icebound

What you'll need: Ice, two spoons, and two buckets

Raid the freezer for ice cubes. Go outdoors and divide the group into two teams. Place a flat tray with the ice cubes on it between the teams, and give the first player on each team a regular spoon.

At the signal, the first two contestants will try to scoop as much ice as possible onto the spoons, carry them to a designated goal, and drop them into a waiting bucket. The players will then return the spoons to the next in line, who repeats the action. If any ice drops, the player must kneel down and scoop it back onto the spoon without using his other hand. The team finishing first wins.

Ice Palace
What you'll need: Various kinds of ice

Let three children at a time take turns building ice palaces. Provide plenty of ice in several varieties, such as ice cubes and crushed ice, so the children can be creative. Allow about two minutes each, then let the next group take turns. If your group is large, you may want to have extra ice available to replace any that melts.

Ice Cream, Lickin' Good
What you'll need: Ice cream, scooper, and paper plates

Ask for several volunteers for this contest and raid the freezer for some ice cream. On individual paper plates place a small uniform size scoop of ice cream. At the signal the contestants will hold their hands behind their backs and use only their tongues to lick their plates clean. No bites allowed! The first one to clean his plate is the winner.

Blizzard Bible Drill
What you'll need: Duplicated worksheet, pencils, and Bibles (King James Version)

Ahead of the party, duplicate the Bible drill for every child expected. Bring along sharpened pencils and Bibles. The children may work alone or in groups of two. Go over the answers when all of them are finished.

Answers:
1. Morsels of ice
2. Plowing
3. Kindle a fire
4. By the breath of God
5. Hailstones
6. Thunder and hail
7. A sycamore

REFRESHMENTS

The guests will have a cold blast raiding the refrigerator to make their own shakes, sodas, or frosts. Set up two or three blenders and make sure helpers are available to supervise. The boys and girls may use the basic recipes suggested and substitute any flavor the "raid" might uncover.

Designate one corner or shelf of the refrigerator and freezer for the children to find a supply of fruit jams, chocolate syrup, milk, lemon-lime soda, frozen orange juice, and vanilla ice cream.

INVITATION

BE A PART OF THE
Frosty Fridge Time!

DATE   TIME   PLACE

Ice Cream Soda
   1 scoop ice cream
   3 Tbsp. milk
   ⅓ cup flavoring (syrup or jam)
   Blend 20 seconds or until smooth and thick. Pour into a glass and fill with lemon-lime soda.

Shake
   3 scoops ice cream
   1 ½ cups milk
   ⅓ cup flavoring (syrup or jam)
   Blend 20 seconds or until smooth and thick. Serve in a tall glass.

Orange Frost
   2 Tbsp. frozen orange juice
   ½ cup cold water
   1 scoop vanilla ice cream
   Blend 30 seconds and pour into a glass.

Serve the drinks with cupcakes or cookies. Appoint a clean-up crew to leave the kitchen in good condition.

DEVOTIONS

Gather the children in a room where they can sit comfortably. Begin the devotional by noting how they have both raided and aided the pastor's refrigerator. This will be an opportunity for you to talk about helping.

Say to the boys and girls that the Bible tells us of young people just like them who also helped others. Refer to John 6:5-13 to remind the students of the boy who gave his lunch to Jesus. Say, **Jesus and the disciples fed about 5,000 people that day. It might not have happened if the boy had not been willing to help Jesus.**

Another story found in II Kings 5 tells about an Israelite servant girl who helped her master. Tell the children, **The girl encouraged Army Commander Naaman to go to Elisha to be healed of leprosy. After washing in the Jordan River seven times, Naaman became clean once again. That couldn't have happened if the girl had not chosen to help him in the first place.**

Ask the students why we should follow these examples and help others when we can. (Helping shows that we are serving the Lord.) Encourage the children to give examples of ways to help.

Repeat the memory verse with the guests, then invite the pastor to pray a benediction.

Blizzard Bible Drill

The Bible includes many verses that talk about the weather or how God has control over the seasons. Look up the following verses to answer the questions.

1. Psalm 147:17—What is hail called in this verse? _____

2. Proverbs 20:4—It was too cold to perform what kind of work? _____

3. Acts 28:1-2—What did the cold weather make the people on the island of Melita do for Paul and the other shipwreck victims? _____

4. Job 37:10—How is frost given? _____

5. Joshua 10:11—What killed many people in Bethhoron? _____

6. Exodus 9:23—What did the Lord send upon the land of Egypt when Moses stretched his rod toward heaven? _____

7. Psalm 78:47—What kind of tree was destroyed by frost? _____

Missions-Minded Progressive Dinner

Memory Verse: "Go ye therefore, and teach all nations."
Matthew 28:19

IDEA
Although it takes a little extra planning, a progressive dinner can make for an exciting evening. The children will experience some interesting foods and customs as well as learn more about what it means to be a missionary.

PUBLICITY
Hang a world map on the meeting room wall or preferably on a cork board. Cut narrow strips of construction paper and use straight pins to outline the group's "itinerary." Start with your hometown, then go on to China, Ireland, Italy, and finally Hawaii. Print the title along a strip of paper and place above the map; print the date, time and place to meet on another sheet and secure at the bottom.

Write in the meeting place, day, and time on the invitation pattern and duplicate.

DECORATIONS & PREPARATION
Find four adults to open their homes for one segment each of the progressive dinner.

Each home should be decorated to represent a different spot on the map. Ask a travel agency for posters advertising each country, and make construction paper flags for each country. More decorating ideas are included below.

If all of the homes aren't within walking distance, make arrangements for transportation.

ACTIVITIES
Experience the Orient: China
What you'll need: Hot tea, mugs, cooked rice, bowls, and forks or chop sticks

At this home the guests can sit on the floor. The home can be decorated with Chinese lanterns, fans, posters of panda bears, etc.

If the weather allows, go outdoors to play "Dragon's Tail." The children will join hands to form a line, one end of which will be the dragon's head and the other his tail. As the dragon weaves back and forth over the playing area, one guest, appointed as "It," will try to tag the person who is the dragon's tail. If he succeeds, the one at the tail becomes the new "It" and the one who caught him goes to be the dragon's head.

Continue playing until the children are ready to settle down for some hot tea and a small bowl of rice. If possible, provide chopsticks and show the children how to use them. You might want to tell your students that for many people, not just in China but all over the world, a bowl of rice is all that is available to eat each day.

Take several minutes to pray for the missions work in China. Ask God to help the missionaries there to be able to share with the people the good news that Jesus can fill their hunger for righteousness.

Before leaving, encourage the boys and girls to thank their hosts by bowing graciously.

More Than Just a Bit of Luck: Ireland
What you'll need: Foil-wrapped chocolate coins, kettle, cream of potato soup, bowls, and spoons

Any decorations you may have on file for St. Patrick's Day, such as green shamrocks or green crepe paper streamers, could be used at this home.

Ahead of time hide foil-wrapped chocolate coins in one room of your host's house. When the children arrive, ask them to help you fill the "Pot of Gold." Give them five minutes to search for the chocolate coins, then have them gather around a large pot to see who has found the most. As the children count, they may drop their coins into the pot. Set it aside for later use in the progressive dinner.

Next the children will enjoy a bowl of soup. What could better represent this country than cream of potato? Explain to the students that potatoes are a very plentiful crop in Ireland.

Talk with the guests about a man who was a missionary to his own country, St. Patrick. Tell them that he used the three-leafed shamrock to help teach the people about the Trinity—that God is the Father, the Son, and the Holy Spirit all in one.

Be sure the students thank their hosts.

Ah, Italia: Italy
What you'll need: Two pieces of paper, two envelopes, individual pizzas or spaghetti with garlic bread, plates, forks, punch, and cups

Use art magazines to find pictures of famous paintings by Italian artists and place these around the room. Red and white checkered tablecloths would also add a nice touch.

Send a "telegram" stating that you'll be back to the United States soon: Divide the group into two teams facing each other. Give the first member of each team an envelope with an identical telegraph message in it. It should consist of at least ten words, such as "Trip around the world almost over. Final destination, _____ home." At the word "go," the leader of each team should read the message silently. He will then whisper the message into the next person's ear. Continue down the line until the last person on each team has received the message. Those students should then run to the host with the message.

The winning team will be the one which delivers the most accurate telegram message, even if that team doesn't come in first. Depending on preparation time and budget concerns, you could serve individual pizzas on hamburger buns, allowing the children to add their own ingredients. Or serve spaghetti with garlic bread and have a contest to see who can slurp a long noodle (without sauce) the fastest. Remember to provide something to drink, such as fruit punch.

If your church is doing any missions work in Italy, take a few minutes to talk to the children about it. A good teaching tool would be pictures of the missionary families.

Have the boys and girls thank their hosts. They can also say, "arrivederci" as they leave.

INVITATION

Come visit exciting lands at the

Missions-Minded Progressive Dinner

Date   Time

Place

Aloha to the United States: Hawaii
What you'll need: Fruit salad and plates

This home can be adorned with greenery and flowers and have soft island music playing in the background. The children would enjoy a real island welcome of a flowery lei to go around their necks. (These can be purchased at a dime store or made from tissue paper or facial tissue.)

You will want to serve the dessert before you finish the rest of the party activities. Fruit salad is a favorite of most youngsters, so mix up bananas, oranges, pineapple tidbits, whipped cream and coconut to make an exotic tropical salad.

REFRESHMENTS

These will have been taken care of at each home.

DEVOTIONS

What you'll need: "Pot of Gold" filled with wrapped chocolates, duplicated Scripture tract, and plastic sandwich bags with ties

Throughout the party, the children's attention will have been directed to the missions. Take this opportunity to discuss the importance of getting the Gospel to the whole world.

Say to the boys and girls, **Though people speak different languages, eat different food and have different customs, the Bible says in Romans 3:23 that everyone is born with a sinful heart. Only the blood of Jesus Christ can make our hearts clean.**

Read to the children the Great Commission given by Jesus in Matthew 28:19-20. Emphasize that the Lord calls all of us to share with others how much God loves us. Whether or not we go to another country, God wants us to help those around us to come to Him.

Read the story of Peter and John's healing of the crippled beggar, found in Acts 3:1-10. Bring out the "pot of gold" filled at the second home with the wrapped chocolates. Let each guest take one to eat, then give each a handful to put in a plastic sandwich bag along with the duplicated Scripture tract. Ask the students to think about a friend or family member who needs to hear the message of God's love. Encourage them to give the filled bag to that person.

Repeat the memory verse with the students. Invite them to pray for the missionaries who are ministering in other countries and for themselves as they try to witness.

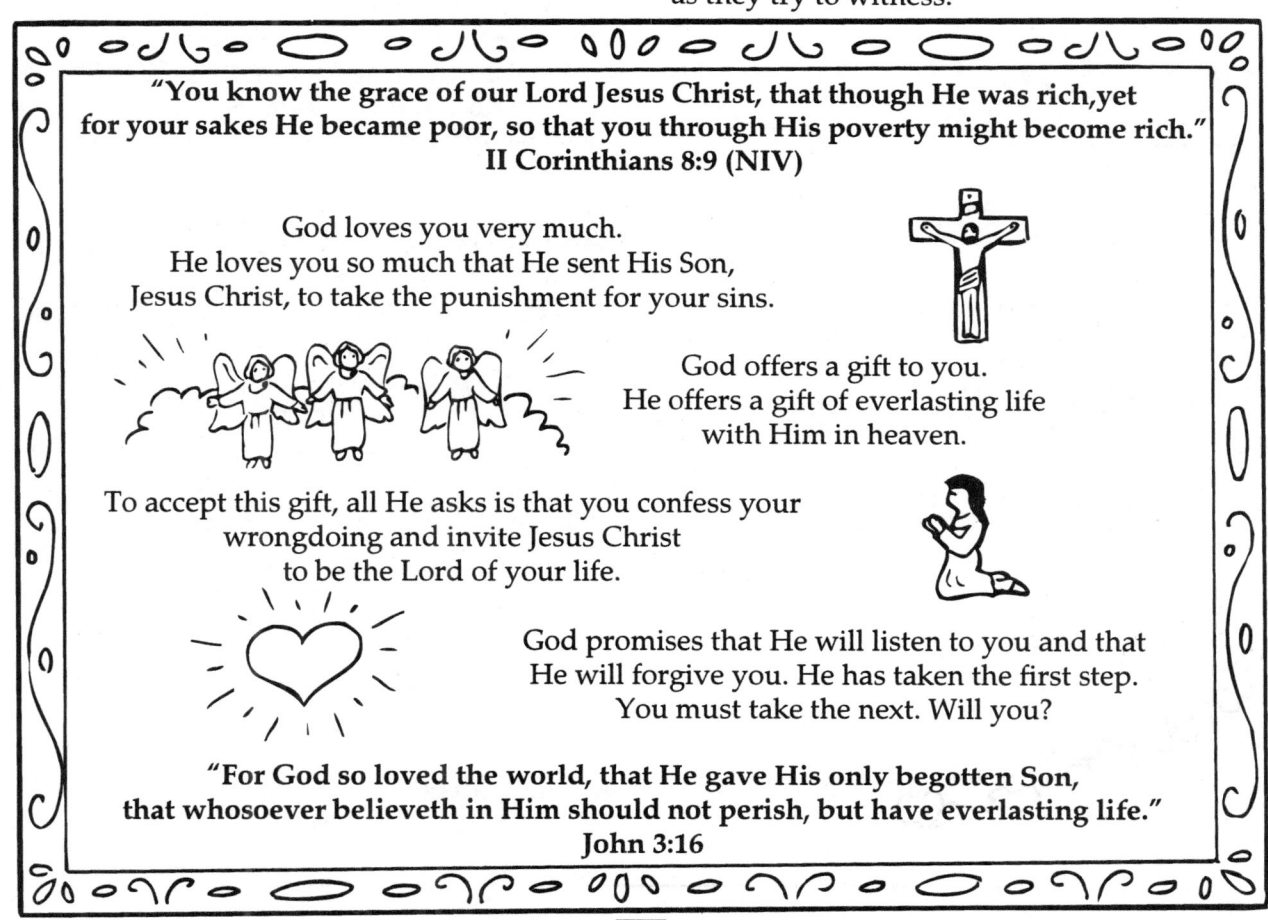

"You know the grace of our Lord Jesus Christ, that though He was rich, yet for your sakes He became poor, so that you through His poverty might become rich."
II Corinthians 8:9 (NIV)

God loves you very much.
He loves you so much that He sent His Son,
Jesus Christ, to take the punishment for your sins.

God offers a gift to you.
He offers a gift of everlasting life
with Him in heaven.

To accept this gift, all He asks is that you confess your
wrongdoing and invite Jesus Christ
to be the Lord of your life.

God promises that He will listen to you and that
He will forgive you. He has taken the first step.
You must take the next. Will you?

"For God so loved the world, that He gave His only begotten Son,
that whosoever believeth in Him should not perish, but have everlasting life."
John 3:16

Jolly Green Jubilee

Memory Verse: "Grow in grace, and in the knowledge of our Lord and Savior Jesus Christ." II Peter 3:18

IDEA With spring comes the green, and that means new life—new leaves, new grass, new flowers, and so on. Help your students welcome spring and at the same time understand that we are called to grow in Christ.

PUBLICITY

Fill in the details on the invitation pattern and duplicate. If you will be handing out the invitations rather than mailing them, glue on a small green leaf.

To make a poster, enlarge the pattern and glue on several large leaves and a flower or two. Make sure to change to fresh greenery if your poster is up for more than a week.

DECORATIONS & PREPARATION

Obviously, green is the way to go in decorating. Green crepe paper strips twisted and strung around the room can alternate with whole sheets of green crepe paper hanging as panels.

Cover windows with green paper if you are meeting during the daytime and wrap the entrance door with green.

If your church has green plants, either live or imitation, check to see if you can borrow them to help decorate the room. Set up a few mixed bouquets around the room, too (give them to your helpers afterward to show your appreciation).

ACTIVITIES

Snatch the Lettuce
What you'll need: Green towel or cloth and yarn or string

This is the same game as the familiar "Steal the Bacon," but with a green touch. Line up the children in two teams on opposite sides of the room. Number the children on both teams so that you have two ones, two twos, two threes, etc. (if the teams are uneven, ask a helper to fill in).

Roll a green towel or cloth into a ball, wind heavy yarn or string around it several times, and then tie a knot to keep the "lettuce" intact. Set the lettuce in the middle of the playing area.

When you call a number, the two children with that number will dash to the middle to "snatch" the lettuce, attempting to bring it back to their own team without being tagged by the other player. Points are scored for successfully snatching the lettuce or for tagging the snatcher. Continue the game until the children are ready for another one. The team with the most points wins green suckers.

How Green You Are
What you'll need: Any object

Have one guest leave the room. While he is gone the group will decide on something he will do when he comes back. They may agree that he is supposed to pull up a window shade, play a tune on the piano, jump on one foot, etc.

When the group calls "Ready" and he returns to the room, the children will start singing, "How green you are, how green you are, how very green you are . . ." to the tune of "Auld Lang Syne" while the one tries to discover what is expected of him. When he gets close to the object involved or nearer to accomplishing the feat, the crowd will sing louder. When he gets farther away, the singing will get softer.

Matching Green
What you'll need: Various shades of green paper and fabric, scissors, a pen, sheets of paper, and pencils

Ahead of time, cut several different sheets of green paper and shades of fabric into two identical pieces. Mount each piece on white paper. Write a number in the corner of one of the pieces and a letter on the other. Hang the matching pieces on opposite sides of the room.

Give each guest a piece of paper and a pencil. When you say "Go," the children should begin moving around the room, trying to match the pieces by writing down the right combination of letters and numbers (such as an apple shape cut from green paper lettered "D" and an apple shape cut from fabric numbered "6." The answer for the match would be D-6).

After five minutes, check papers to see who is the most accurate. Award these with green candy or mints.

Which Green Is Greenwich?
What you'll need: Duplicated matching quiz and pencils
Let the students work in pairs on this matching quiz, which you will have duplicated ahead of time. The first couple to finish with the most correct answers can be awarded green pencils.

Answers:
1. h   2. c   3. b   4. e
5. a   6. f   7. d   8. g

REFRESHMENTS
Follow the color scheme and serve some green treats—choose from cake or cupcakes with green frosting, lime gelatin, green mint ice cream, green frosted cookies, etc. Serve with green fruit drink.

DEVOTIONS
With the guests sitting down for the devotional, talk about all the activities that have been related to green. Point out the green decorations and note that green stands for growth. Spring brings a lot of green, as it is the time when the trees get their leaves again and the flowers start to bloom.

Ask the children, **How do people show that they are physically growing?** (Our hair gets longer, we need bigger clothes, etc.) **What do we need in order to grow?** (Nutritional food, plenty of fluids, exercise, and sleep.)

Explain to the students that as Christians, we

INVITATION

It's a Jolly Green Jubilee!

DATE   TIME   PLACE

know that God has planned special ways for us to grow spiritually as well. God says each child of God needs to grow, and He wants us to grow to be more and more like His Son, Jesus.

Read Ephesians 4:15 and ask, **What are some ways that we can show we are growing spiritually?** (Show more kindness, be a helper, memorize Scripture, etc.) Encourage the boys and girls to suggest what we need in order to grow spiritually (this could include regular personal reading of the Bible, prayer, studying the Bible with others, and sharing the Good News with others).

Say the memory verse with the children. Have an open prayer time so they may each have an opportunity to ask God to help them grow.

Which Green Is Greenwich?
Matching Quiz

Read through the two lists below to try to decide which definition matches the "green" word. Write the correct letter on the line next to the number.

_____	1. Greenhouse	a.	Jealous
_____	2. Green	b.	An Arctic country
_____	3. Greenland	c.	Before a piece of fruit is ripe
_____	4. Green thumb	d.	A professional football team
_____	5. Green with envy	e.	One who likes to care for plants
_____	6. Green bean	f.	A vegetable
_____	7. Green Bay Packers	g.	A place for practicing golf
_____	8. Putting green	h.	A building where plants are grown

Planting Project

Memory Verse: "The fruit of the Spirit is love, joy, peace, patience, kindness, goodness, faithfulness, gentleness and self-control." Galatians 5:22-23 (NIV)

IDEA
This get-together doubles as an opportunity to decorate potted plants as gifts and a chance to play fun games that have to do with planting. Your students will also discover what kind of crop is expected of the Christian's "garden."

PUBLICITY
Fill in the details on the invitation pattern and duplicate for the guests. Enlarge the pattern to make a poster, decorating it with pictures of fruits and vegetables cut out from old magazines or with packets of seeds.

DECORATIONS & PREPARATION
Make arrangements of a variety of vegetables and fruits to place in bowls around the room and especially on the serving table.

Set up work tables for the "Planting Project." This will be a special task designed to cheer the students' mothers (as for Mother's Day) or people from the church who are shut-ins. If you decide to give the plants to people who are shut-ins, make arrangements for the boys and girls to go to their homes and deliver them personally. It might be best to do this directly after the meeting when all the children are still present.

ACTIVITIES

Planting Project
What you'll need: Small potted plants, aluminum foil, tape, ribbon, craft sticks, construction paper, and pens

The children will decorate potted plants as gifts for their mothers and/or the elderly.

Set out all the materials on work tables. Show the children how to make "double-sided" rolls of tape and secure these in several places around the planter. Instruct the guests to lay a sheet of foil wrap, colored side down, on the table and set the planter in the middle. Gather the wrap around the planter, smoothing over the rolls of tape. Tie a ribbon around the planter and make a big bow.

The children may write special messages on construction paper and tape these to the tops of craft sticks. Help them insert the craft sticks into the soil.

Bean Bucket
What you'll need: A bucket and several beanbags

Place a bucket against the wall. Use yarn or string to mark five lines at three-foot intervals, starting several feet from the bucket and moving away from it.

Line up the players off to the side. Starting from the closest line, the contestants will take turns throwing beanbags into the bucket. When successful, they may move backward to the next line and continue until they miss. The next player will start at the closest line.

Fruit Basket Upset
What you'll need: Circle of chairs

Here's a traditional favorite that children usually enjoy. Place chairs in a circle—enough for every child but one, who will take his place in the center as "It." Instead of numbering, give each player the name of a fruit. Several students should have the same fruit name.

When "It" calls out the name of a fruit, all the players with that name must scramble to exchange chairs while "It" tries to find a seat. The one who is left out then becomes the new "It" and play continues. When "It" calls "Fruit basket upset!" everyone changes places.

Hot Potato
What you'll need: Circle of chairs, a timer or watch with

a second hand, and a potato

Play this traditional game by having the students sit in a circle and start passing a potato as quickly as possible. When time runs out, whoever is holding the potato is out. The last one in the circle is the winner. Award him a coupon for french fries from a local restaurant.

Hidden Harvest Puzzle
What you'll need: Duplicated puzzle and pencils

Duplicate the word puzzle before the party, making sure to cover the answer box first. Let each child work for about ten minutes. The children may continue working until it is time for devotions.

REFRESHMENTS

Provide a "buffet" of various raw vegetables and fruits along with juice to drink. A carrot cake with cream cheese frosting would make a just-right dessert.

DEVOTIONS

Let the children themselves give the devotional. Divide the group into four teams and explain that they will be planting a Christian garden. Provide paper and pencils.

(1) Team One will plant the "peas" for the garden. Give the students the following Scripture references to find Christ-like characteristics that begin with a "p":

James 5:7—patience; Isaiah 26:3—peace; I Thessalonians 5:17—pray; Hebrews 13:20-21—perfect; and I John 3:22—pleasing.

(2) Team Two will look up things that we should "squash," or get rid of, in the Christian garden:

Proverbs 29:23—pride; James 3:6-8—(an evil) tongue; Ephesians 4:31—bitterness, wrath, anger, clamour, evil speaking malice; Song of Solomon 8:6—jealousy; and Proverbs 31:27—idleness.

(3) Team Three's task will be to plant the "lettuce" for followers of Christ:

I Thessalonians 5:6—"Let us watch and be sober;" Galatians 6:10—"Let us do good unto all men;" Romans 13:13—"Let us walk honestly;" I John 3:18—"Let us not love in word, neither in tongue; but in deed and in truth."

When the groups are finished, let them share their answers with the rest of the group. Say the memory verse together and close in prayer.

INVITATION

BE A PART OF THE Planting Project!

DATE TIME PLACE

Hidden Harvest Puzzle

Farmer Williams is having trouble keeping track of all the vegetables in his garden. Can you help? There are twelve vegetables hidden across, down, backward, and diagonally. Draw a circle around the words when you find them, then mark them off on the list.

BEET	BROCCOLI	CABBAGE	CARROT
CELERY	CORN	LETTUCE	ONION
PEA	RADISH	SPINACH	TOMATO

Hidden Harvest Puzzle

```
L K B I I K X G D Y J G M B I V N Q L R Z C
E F M T Q B R O C C O L I Z V C S B K X M V
K X S E Z Y F J R E F N J V X W I N G K R D
R T M E M O B W K R M Q E P V T H K T L H F
Z V I B S M P T C M Y S I Y F P F L K O R R
H Q A Q V M L V A S H L Z G L E E S S R T D
L M E K C L O N I O N S Y P O A L U Q I D J
C X C D B I D Z E S A H Q C H F X Y E H E C
R A U G S J D G O D C Q P M H X Y O G K B V
K M T W K L B Q L K P K K Y R L A M A W Y W
V H T X S L L V K F U R Y V T Y E E B R Z O
R C E X N V Z F W F S T L L D C B X B L K H
C S L T S Q P Z V T I V G V S P I N A C H J
W X O V O D B S V K W Z F E S A Z D C U K P
N I G J L M Z P X W O U U D G T O R R A C E
R P W A U Q A I T I G C J N C O O Z Q R M S
O O N R D L F T R T J Z N F U Q U N I F Y T
C H R Y X P Z K O R Q F M N J X R A D I S H
E V W C N C E L E R Y P L E Z A G Q G C V O
```

Answers:

```
L K B I I K X G D Y J G M B I V N Q L R Z C
E F M T Q B R O C C O L I Z V C S B K X M V
K X S E Z Y F J R E F N J V X W I N G K R D
R T M E M O B W K R M Q E P V T H K T L H F
Z V I B S M P T C M Y S I Y F P F L K O R R
H Q A Q V M L V A S H L Z G L E E S S R T D
L M E K C L O N I O N S Y P O A L U Q I D J
C X C D B I D Z E S A H Q C H F X Y E H E C
R A U G S J D G O D C Q P M H X Y O G K B V
K M T W K L B Q L K P K K Y R L A M A W Y W
V H T X S L L V K F U R Y V T Y E E B R Z O
R C E X N V Z F W F S T L L D C B X B L K H
C S L T S Q P Z V T I V G V S P I N A C H J
W X O V O D B S V K W Z F E S A Z D C U K P
N I G J L M Z P X W O U U D G T O R R A C E
R P W A U Q A I T I G C J N C O O Z Q R M S
O O N R D L F T R T J Z N F U Q U N I F Y T
C H R Y X P Z K O R Q F M N J X R A D I S H
E V W C N C E L E R Y P L E Z A G Q G C V O
```

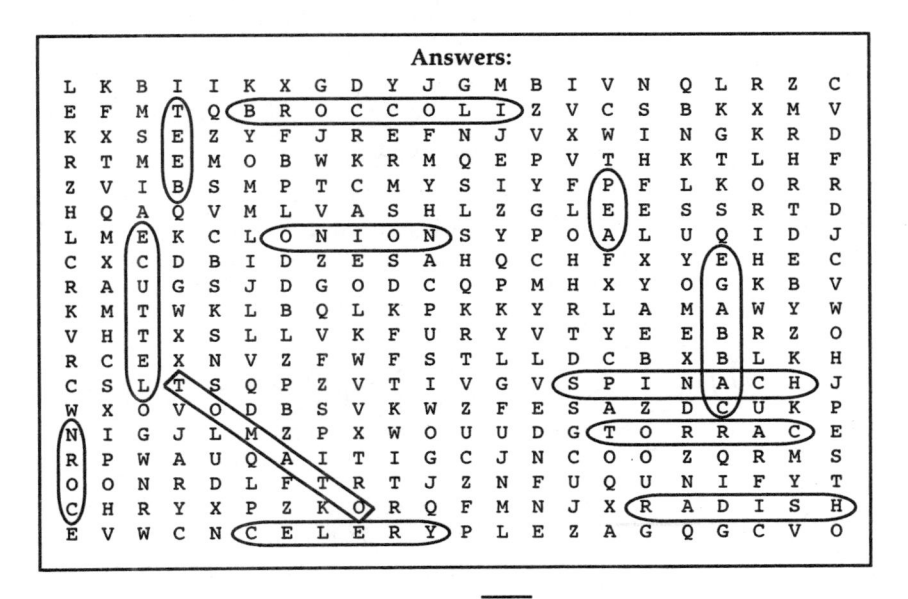

61

Traffic Jam-Boree

Memory Verse: "Watch and pray, that ye enter not into temptation." Matthew 26:41

IDEA
Of course your students cannot drive, but they do know what it means to follow directions. The activities included here will remind them to pay close attention to instructions from the Lord and from others!

PUBLICITY
Duplicate the pattern to make invitations, filling in the date, time, and place.

You may enlarge the invitation pattern to make posters or make a "traffic-stopping" poster yourself. Cut out large circles from red, yellow, and green paper and glue in the appropriate spots on a sheet of black poster board. Write TRAFFIC JAM-BOREE on a strip of white paper placed at the top and include the details on the colored circles.

DECORATIONS & PREPARATION
Duplicate the STOP, YIELD, and ONE WAY patterns several times onto red, yellow, and white construction paper, respectively, and hang these in various spots around the room. Keep one set to use for devotion time.

Plan to hold the event in a large indoor area so the children have room to move around.

ACTIVITIES

Three Deep
What you'll need: Room to play

Have the children form a circle, two deep, facing the center. Two players on the outside of the circle will begin the game as runner and chaser. The runner may save himself from being tagged by stepping in front of one of the pairs of players, making the circle three deep at that point. The outside player must immediately leave or be tagged. If a player is tagged, he becomes the chaser.

A runner may run in any direction he chooses, to the right or left or across the circle. However, he can only step in front of a player and make the circle three deep by moving into the circle from the outside and to the right.

Streets and Alleys
What you'll need: Room to play

Only one student will be chased in this game of tag, but all the others will make it difficult for him!

Group the children in rows so that they will stand with their fingertips just touching when they hold their hands out. Then, when they turn ninety degrees, have them placed so that the fingers of each person will reach to the elbow on the arm of the one to each side of him. Select one student as the leader and choose two others to be the chaser and the chased.

The game will begin by everyone standing with arms outstretched, touching fingers with the one next to him. Those who are playing tag will begin running the "alleys" formed by the outstretched arms. The runner is not permitted to break through.

When the leader calls out, "Streets!" all the children will drop their arms for a moment and make a quarter turn to the right, then immediately join arms again, this time with different players. They will change again in the same manner when the leader calls, "Alleys!"

Design Engineers
What you'll need: Two large sheets of blank paper, masking tape, and pens

Tape the two pieces of paper at the children's shoulder level on a wall, several feet apart. Divide the group into two teams. When you give the signal, the line leaders are to come forward and draw a "freeway scene" (cars, the road, exit signs, etc.) on their team's sheet. After ten seconds, signal the next players in line to take a turn. Continue until all the players have had a chance to draw. Determine the winning team by the quality of the picture.

Red Light, Green Light
What you'll need: Room to play

This traditional favorite fits in well with the traffic theme.

Select a child to be the leader; the rest of the students will stand at a starting line across the room. The leader begins with his back facing the players and says, "Green light!" The children quickly take as many steps as they can before the leader turns to face them and says, "Red light!" They must stay "frozen" until he turns his back and gives another green light. If they anticipate or lose balance, they are out of the game. The first one to reach the leader takes his place for the next round.

REFRESHMENTS

Decorate sugar cookies with red, yellow, and green icing and serve with fruit punch or milk.

DEVOTIONS

If you have words available or your students already know it, sing "Stop, and Let Me Tell You."

Hold up the signs made ahead of time (see Preparation) and ask the children, **Did you know that God gives us directions like these?**

Read Ephesians 4:27 and hold up the STOP sign. Ask, **What does it mean to not "give place" to the devil?** (Don't give him the chance to confuse you or make wrong choices.) **How can we stop doing what is wrong?** Read II Chronicles 30:8 and hold up the YIELD sign. **What does it mean to yield ourselves to the LORD?** (To let Him help us make the right choices.)

Read John 14:6 and hold up the ONE WAY sign. **Is it enough just to "yield" to God?** (No, we must accept Jesus as our Savior, asking Him to forgive our sins, because He is the only true way to come to know God.) Read I John 1:9, emphasizing that God will forgive us when we ask Him to.

Point out to the children that we need to pay attention to the Lord's directions if we are going to follow Him successfully. Say the memory verse with the children, then offer a closing prayer with them, asking God to help them know to watch and listen.

INVITATION

It's a Traffic Jam-Boree!

STOP WONDERING WHAT TO DO— JUST COME!

DATE   TIME   PLACE

PATTERNS FOR DUPLICATION

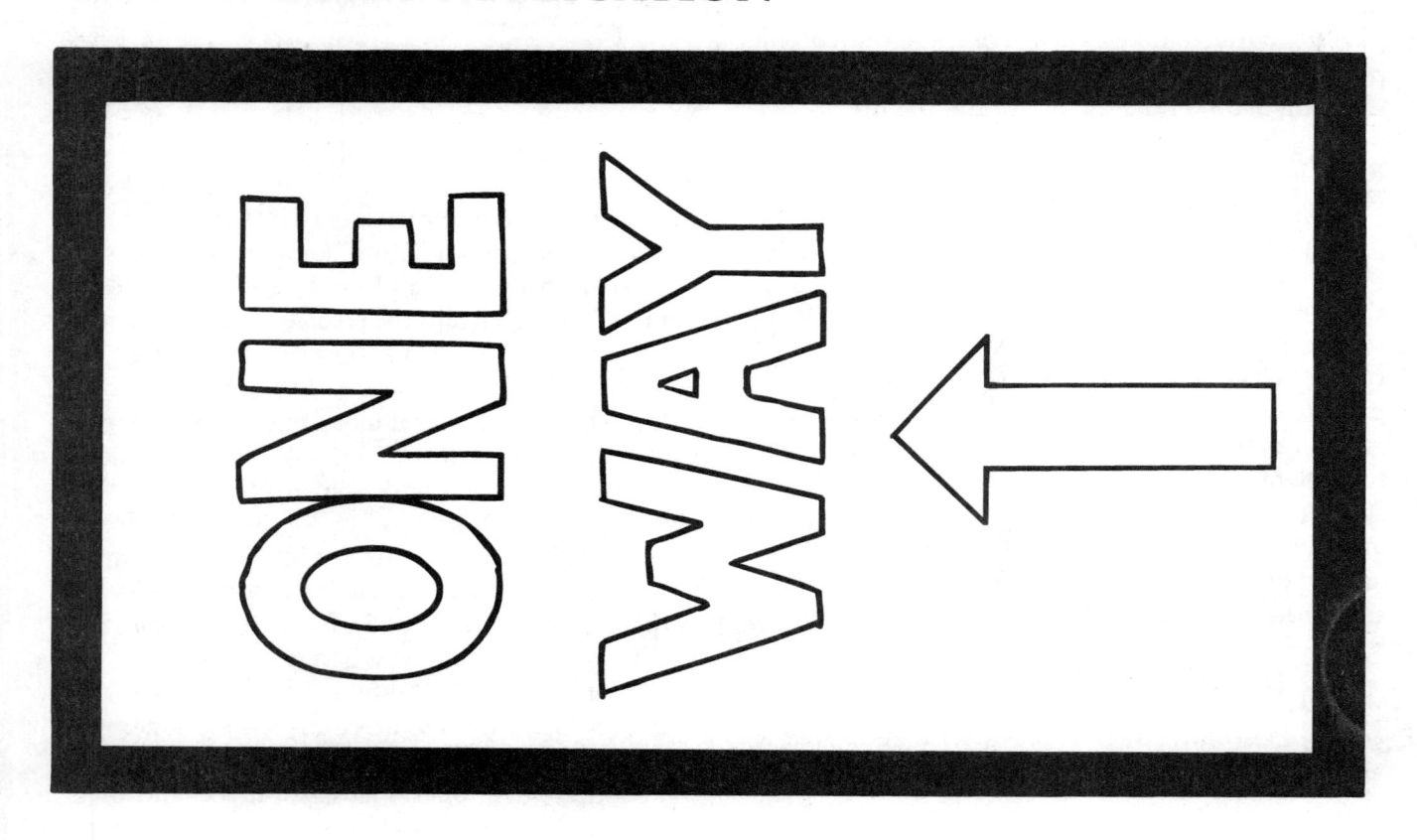

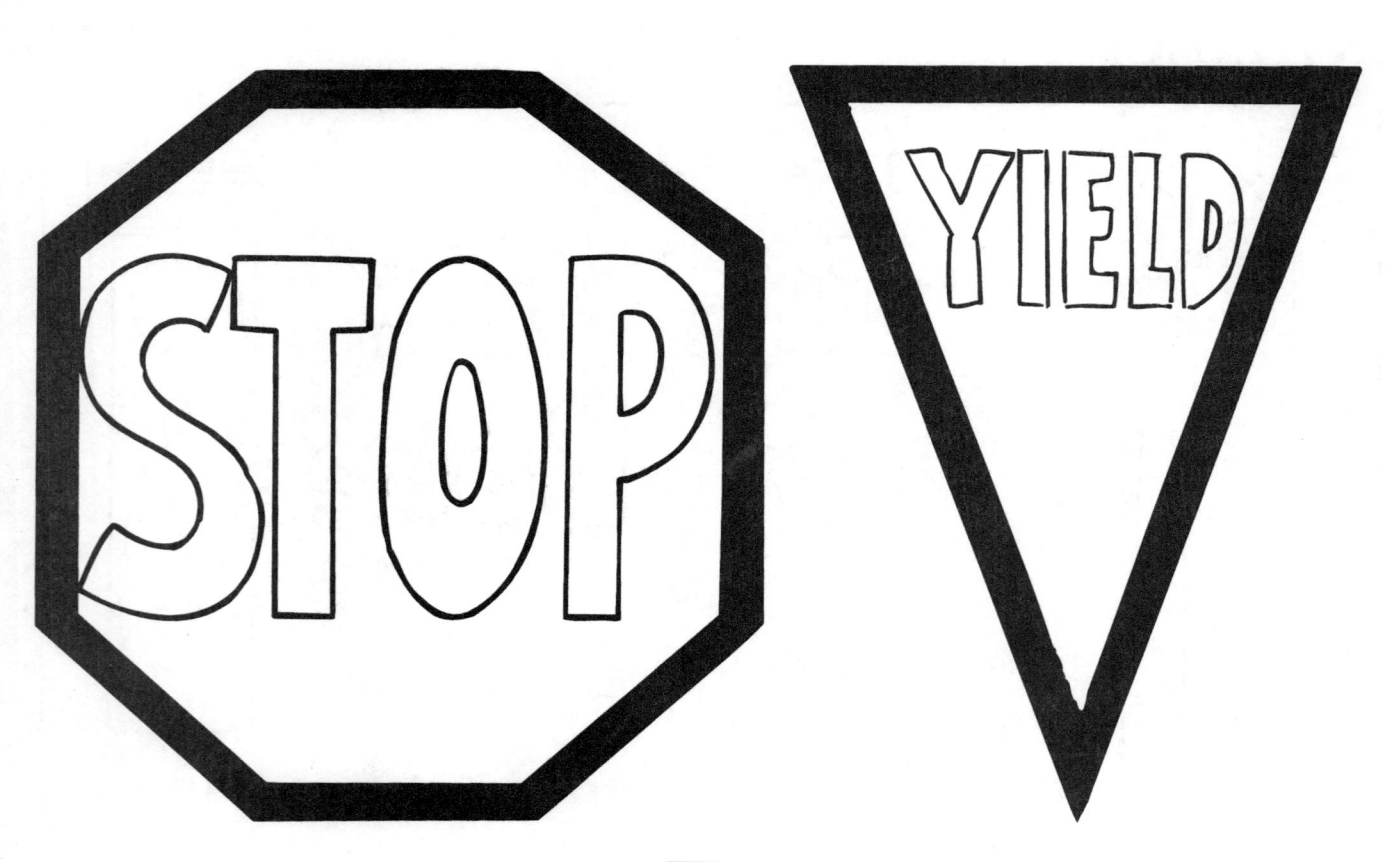